T0121043

HONOR TO THE GREAT HEAD OF THE CHURCH

A Transformational Model for Church Leadership, Administration, and Management

TRANSFORMATIONAL CHURCH ADMINISTRATION SERIES

Volume One

Margarette W. Williams, Ed.D., Ph.D.

FOREWORD BY DR. GEOFFREY VAN GUNS

WESTBOW
P R E S S®
A DIVISION OF THOMAS NELSON
& ZONDERVAN

Copyright © 2021 Margarette W. Williams, Ed.D., Ph.D.

All rights reserved. No part of this book may be used or reproduced by any means, graphic, electronic, or mechanical, including photocopying, recording, taping or by any information storage retrieval system without the written permission of the author except in the case of brief quotations embodied in critical articles and reviews.

This book is a work of non-fiction. Unless otherwise noted, the author and the publisher make no explicit guarantees as to the accuracy of the information contained in this book and in some cases, names of people and places have been altered to protect their privacy.

WestBow Press books may be ordered through booksellers or by contacting:

WestBow Press
A Division of Thomas Nelson & Zondervan
1663 Liberty Drive
Bloomington, IN 47403
www.westbowpress.com
844-714-3454

Because of the dynamic nature of the Internet, any web addresses or links contained in this book may have changed since publication and may no longer be valid. The views expressed in this work are solely those of the author and do not necessarily reflect the views of the publisher, and the publisher hereby disclaims any responsibility for them.

Any people depicted in stock imagery provided by Getty Images are models, and such images are being used for illustrative purposes only.
Certain stock imagery © Getty Images.

Scripture marked (KJV) taken from the King James Version of the Bible.

Scripture marked (NKJV) taken from the New King James Version®. Copyright © 1982 by Thomas Nelson. Used by permission. All rights reserved.

Scripture quotations marked (NIV) are taken from the Holy Bible, New International Version®, NIV®. Copyright © 1973, 1978, 1984, 2011 by Biblica, Inc.® Used by permission of Zondervan. All rights reserved worldwide. www.zondervan.com The "NIV" and "New International Version" are trademarks registered in the United States Patent and Trademark Office by Biblica, Inc.®

Scripture quotations marked (ESV) are from The ESV® Bible (The Holy Bible, English Standard Version®), copyright © 2001 by Crossway, a publishing ministry of Good News Publishers. Used by permission. All rights reserved.

Scripture quotations marked (NASB) taken from the (NASB®) New American Standard Bible®, Copyright © 1960, 1971, 1977, 1995, 2020 by The Lockman Foundation. Used by permission. All rights reserved. www.lockman.org"

Scripture quotations marked (NLT) are taken from the Holy Bible, New Living Translation, copyright ©1996, 2004, 2015 by Tyndale House Foundation. Used by permission of Tyndale House Publishers, Carol Stream, Illinois 60188. All rights reserved.

ISBN: 978-1-6642-3889-3 (sc)
ISBN: 978-1-6642-3890-9 (hc)
ISBN: 978-1-6642-3891-6 (e)

Library of Congress Control Number: 2021913240

Print information available on the last page.

WestBow Press rev. date: 08/03/2021

DEDICATION

Dedicated to the memory of the people who gave me life, my parents, Eunice and Dorothy Williams. My father was solidly balanced. My mother was unbroken. One of her most memorable sayings taught me to seek truth for all of life. It was simply, "Daughter, singing and shouting is fine; but you must live this life!"

A Sister's Review

"After reading the first twenty-nine pages, you have shared a Transformational Model for (1) Leadership, (2) Administration, and (3) Management with pastors and other church leaders in this book. Your book should be a new paradigm shift for the contemporary church. Beginning with the first sentence in the opening paragraph, the movement in this book should be toward a new model for the existing church. Your book presents thinking outside the current, predictable assessment in leadership, administration, and management. The preceding is my thinking about this book. The structure is phenomenal."

Sentiments provided by
Dr. Bettye J. Williams, PhD
Pine Bluff, AR

ACKNOWLEDGEMENTS

Gratitude! As I think of completing the writing of this endeavor to express my appreciation for all Christ has been in my life, in the life of the church, and what His coming means for the world, I sum it with no better word than *gratitude*. Actually, I do not have wise expressions, nor do I possess grand or lofty sayings to adequately give voice to how, at this moment, I so love God for all He has allowed me to accomplish with this assignment.

Completing such a weighty undertaking was indeed a mission, a duty, and a responsibility. In my opinion, its scope to advance new thought for current and historical literature in leadership and administration for the church is substantial. Thank you Father for allowing me to pursue it, to examine required research to the end and yes, for giving me *GRACE* to complete it. My most thoughtful words of appreciation are insufficient, so I will simply shout a "thankful cry of hallelujah!"

Heartfelt thanks to my husband, Lewis, for his unwavering love for me. From day one of his meeting me, he immediately assumed his God ordained role to look after me, to protect me, care for me, and to shield me from the many darts of life's shooting arrows. His courageous strength has kept me going when I, on my own, would have given in and given up on much that God sent for us to accomplish.

Special thanks to my two amazing daughters, Marceinia (Gregory) and Lyska (Terrance). They somehow have decided to combine the love they share for their parents to form a unit of quiet fortitude and together, they are now a towering fortress of power and strength to undergird us through the many places in life God has chosen to take us. So beautiful are their precious souls and also the hearts of their adoringly devoted husbands, our two sons in love. To my grandsons Malcolm, Jordan, Jayden, and Johnathan, I thank God for the men he gave to our legacy. To my tenacious Maya, my strong and favorite granddaughter, continue to be you!

To my sisters and brothers, Evester L. Darrough (deceased), Dr. Bettye J. Williams, Shirley M. Williams, Dr. Brenda F. Graham, Charles L. Williams (deceased), N. Lucille Gilkey, Sterlin (Priscilla) D. Williams, Ted W. Williams, Robin N. Baylock, and Sonnya (Dwight) Adams, thank you for being the family I needed. Thank you to Dr. Bettye, Dr. Brenda, and Shirley for providing "fresh eyes" and valuable commentary to the manuscript.

Special appreciation to my dear friend, Nettye Johnson of Baton Rouge, LA for giving careful directives and inspiring critique during the early days to get this work off the drawing board. Your meticulous guidance and gentle nudging put me on the right path to pulling this work out from my heart and on to the pages of print.

ACKNOWLEDGEMENTS
TO CONTRIBUTING PASTORS

Seven Pastors from the Arkansas Regular and Consolidated Baptist State Conventions contributed to the writing of Chapter Five, *"The Pastor: God's Agent as Church Leader."* While I am filled with gratitude to pursue and complete this study in church leadership, administration, and management, I acknowledge that I have not been called to the office of pastor. After seeking spiritual guidance to adequately present the work of a pastor in this timely volume of study, I felt led to ask pastors to assist me with Chapter Five. I therefore sought out pastors from within the Arkansas church conventions to contribute their support for the process.

The procedure to include pastors began with a *Letter of Consent to Participate* in an eight-question survey from each pastor. Ten pastors were invited; the seven pastors listed below returned their forms with signature documentation to confirm their participation. Four pastors returned written responses and three pastors dictated their answers via a recording. A special *thank you* to express my appreciation for your contribution is extended to each of you.

Pastor Glenn Barnes
Pine Hill Baptist Church, Pine Bluff, AR

Pastor Brian Castle
Indiana Street Baptist Church, Pine Bluff, AR

Pastor Derick L. Easter
New St. Hurricane Baptist Church, Pine Bluff, AR

Pastor Amelio P. Howard
Grace Temple Baptist Church, Pine Bluff, AR

Pastor Ronald Laurent
First Missionary Baptist Church, Holly Grove, AR

Pastor Gardiner L. Sanders
Mercy Seat Baptist Church, Little Rock, AR

Pastor Roderick Smith
Centennial Baptist Church – Kensett, AR

Thank You
Lola Thrower, Little Rock, AR
Edits and Review

I have known Dr. Margarette W. Williams for more than twenty-five years. We have worked together as Christian Educators in the National Baptist Congress of Christian Education and with the Sunday School Publishing Board of the National Baptist Convention, U.S.A., Inc. In 2018 she shared with me this idea she had about writing a book on leadership. Her vision has come alive in this book. For forty-two years, I have had a keen interest in understanding why some church leaders are highly effective and others seem not to ever get off the ground. During our conversation, Dr. Williams shared with me her interest in writing about the leadership responsibilities of the pastor of the local church. Her goal, as she explained it to me, was to highlight the importance of the pastor's leadership of insuring that the church was mission-focused and mission-minded.

HONOR to the Great Head of the Church; A Transformational Model for Leadership, Administration and Management is a book that deserves to be a part of every church leader's library. Who is the Great Head of the Church? It is Jesus Christ, who has commissioned the church to preach the gospel to the ends of the earth. In this groundbreaking work, she focuses on Leadership, Administration, and Management. This trilogy of responsibilities provides the pillars for building and leading an effective congregational ministry. Dr. Williams begins by establishing a theological framework for mission and ministry of the church. She states the "Bible is the undeniable source for truth and Divine Light." At the center of everything is the Sovereign Lord who guides and directs the work of the local church.

Dr. Williams methodically weaves her experiences and intellect into a well-written and timely work that will influence leaders and churches for decades. Each chapter builds upon the firm biblical foundation of God's sovereignty. The cross is the central message of the church, and it is the guiding light of the church's mission. At the core of Dr. Williams' work is the importance of being clear about our purpose. As someone who has studied, taught, and written about congregational leadership, this book is a must read. Those of us who seek to lead the people of God in the work of missions and ministry are indebted to Dr. Margarette W. Williams for such a major contribution.

Geoffrey Van Guns
State Director of Christian Education
Virginia Baptist State Convention

CONTENTS

INTRODUCTION

I absolutely love ministry leadership. If there was only one profession in life to live, for me it would be that of growing and guiding God's people to reaching their fullest potential in kingdom living. It is my calling to help others make choices leading to righteous living for eternal life. A business entrepreneurial model was God's design in ministry for my family and my life.

Thirty-six years of service in leadership management in the church and community brings with it some amazing and eye-opening experiences. Obviously, there are equal numbers, if not more, of challenges associated with designing and constructing a life in ministry.

Far too many ministry obligations can become overwhelming, even downright distracting from God's grand purpose. There are times when the missional message of the cross is circumvented by far too many nonrelated causes and circumstances, most of them having very little value to God's message for His church. The purpose for our charge to labor can become secondary to daily obligations and adjustments to rigorous scheduling. Depending on the stressors and how we relate to them, we may even forget why we committed to working in the vineyard in the first place.

Ministry leaders from multiple service models are called upon, as a result of this reading, to encourage themselves daily. The desire to stay on Christ's message of redemption must rise out of a focused commitment to remain grounded and faithful to His purpose.

I invite you to engage the message of this practical, yet inspiring guide book, HONOR *To The Great Head of the Church: A Transformational Model for Church Leadership, Administration, and Management*. The expectations from this volume are that it will give renewed perspectives to hold fast to our Lord's devotion in every matter of church organization. This steadfast devotion must come from ministry leaders, congregational members and even in personal stewardship to the church.

HONOR to the Great Head of the Church has at its core one central message. That message is that Christ is God's mission. Christ is His *only* mission for the Church. As our Lord delivered Christ to the church, we, His Ambassadors, join Him to carry Christ to the world. New converts in turn share in His glorious acts of redemption and discipleship. Our commission is that we strive daily to grow as one body *in* Christ.

Beginning in February, 1985, accepting God's will to serve others with the gospel message through Christian bookstore operations has been part of the journey God tailored for my life. Since that time, I have served as a teacher, a director, and a dean in Christian Education. This included many years as a director of church ministries, education director and as a dean for numerous Christian leadership schools and congresses. For utmost growth, teaching, training, and mentoring have regularly been part of the works of service assigned to me as a director and leader in ministry.

There have been so many moving parts associated with this voyage, far too numerous to place in this introduction. But if I were to choose one of the numerous times I knew God was perfecting a new pathway for my life, it was the day I read Christopher J. H. Wright's *The Mission of God*.[1] Perusing Wright's book changed my life. It enlightened my spirit and my understanding of church and mission. Actually, I have not been the same since.

Why I was led to study that exhaustive work is not as relevant to today's point as the message God delivered to me on the day of the first read. Wright's insight of scripture and of God's mission for mankind was of profound significance to my personal journey. I was convinced that there needed to exist an urgency to seek and to genuinely serve Him in a more passionate way.

The message totally transformed my thinking. My conceptualization of who I was in Christ was awakened in a way I had not previously discovered. The fact that God was revealing Himself in this manner was a tremendous renewal. Because of His grace, He has continued to share more mysteries of His love for me over and over again. I call these "new mercies" I receive day by day. For this cause, I am more than determined to give *ear* to hear His voice for the church and its impact in the kingdom.

Participating in the Act of Christ

Christopher Wright wrote in *The Mission of God* that "God does not have a mission for the church but rather, He desires a church for His mission."[2] He proceeded to shed light on the difference between God's mission and the mission of His people. *Mission* is the meaning and message of the church. Christians must know that the church exists *only* as it is *in mission*. The church exists as it participates in the "Act of Christ." Who is Christ? Christ is the Great Head of the church; God's mission and His mandate for the church.

Jesus Christ is the mission of the Church! The mission of God was that He sent His Son into the world to die as a ransom for our sin and redeem us to Him. Without Christ, we are utterly lost. We are lost in all things spiritual.

There can be no church without the redeemer as its mission. We only exist as we carry Christ to the world. Thus, we become connected to God's mission as we are sent from Him, by Him. We become *partakers in God's mission* to reconcile the world to Him. With Christ, we are the church on behalf of the King for others. Everyone and all things for our Lord, Christ!

It is my desire that this book communicates the necessity to combine God's mission from biblical theology with principles of organizational leadership and management for an application leading to transformational administration in ministry. Parts of the literature research were gathered from the works of authors and experts in the fields of leadership, management, and administration. Many of whom are also researchers and authors in religion, education, industry, and business management.

Contents

The content of Volume One, *HONOR To the Great Head of the Church; A Transformational Model for Leadership, Administration, and Management* will outline four major categories of church ministry: God's Mission and His Sovereignty, Leadership, Administration, and Management.

The study presents what I believe will be a new positional statement, a renewed model in fact and details and a rekindled focus for thought to the modern-day delivery in the messaging of God's mission for the local church.

Theories in organizational systems management paired with doctrine from scripture will intersect to form a foundational premise for how God's Word connects the two to produce excellence in methods of ministry for the transformational church. A design model connecting truths from God's Word to concepts in organizational theory is significant to illustrate how God has constructed systems of order to the management of His mission for the church. The scientific nature of organizational systems management is evidence that God uses many constructs in life to accomplish His purpose for His people. The case for a transformative church reality in the work of the kingdom will be presented throughout the twelve chapters of this volume.

Each section of the text will highlight subtopics and headings descriptive of that area of ministry. These headings include servant and transformational leadership, discipleship, teaching, fellowship, service, mentoring, team building, and transitioning. Church administration and management will coalesce with theories of organizational development to highlight current approaches found in church administrative functions. Essential ideas for grasping a fuller understanding of all sections presented are included to guide readers to further appreciate their worthiness for the church.

Scripture paired with application and examples will help readers maintain a biblical commitment to retain focus for a deeper reverence to God. The core of the study serves to direct all worship, all admiration, and all HONOR in kingdom worship toward Christ, who is God's grand mission to redeem lost man. This single-minded purpose of the church will be highlighted throughout the text.

SECTION ONE

Transforming God's Church for His Mission

CHAPTER ONE

The Sovereignty of God

God's Divine Sovereignty

From the beginning, the Bible has been man's undeniable source of truth and divine light. God's holy scripture is declaration of the immutable sovereignty of God. Divine sovereignty is the dominant idea running throughout all foundational themes of the Bible. From the Book of Genesis[3] to the final declaration of Christ's ultimate triumph in the Book of Revelation, the all supremacy of God is declared for everyone to know and receive Him. From the first writings of the Pentateuch to the last book of eschatology; from the beginning to the end, the Bible is the absolute record of God's relationship with man. The Bible declares His work in redemption from the curse. It proclaims His deliverance for salvation at the cross of Christ and the resurrection.

The sovereignty of God or divine sovereignty is described in scripture as the doctrine for believer's faith and the eternal security of believers. God's ultimate goal was for man's achievement of "no more death or sorrow" as found in Revelation 21:4, (NLT). It is Christian doctrine that God is the supreme authority and the Great Head of the church. All things of life are under His control. God is the "sovereign Lord of all by an incontestable right [as the] creator, owner and possessor of heaven and earth." Sovereignty is an attribute of God based upon the premise that God, as the creator of heaven and earth, has absolute right and full authority to do or allow whatever He desires. [4]

In his thought-provoking essay, "The Sovereignty of God," John Piper [5] shares views of what it means to be God. In Isaiah 46:9 (ESV), God says "I am God, and there is no other: I am God, and there is none like me." In the context of the text from verse nine, God responds to all of life with a resounding "I am God!" In verse ten He uses two statements to make the declaration:

First, "I declare that things turn out long before they ever happen; second, I declare that for not just natural events, but also human events---doings, things that are not yet done. I know what these things will be long before they have come to pass."

God continues to express His sovereignty by stating in verse ten b that,

"I declare the end from the beginning and from ancient times, things that are not yet accomplished; my counsel shall stand, and I will bring forth all my purpose."

Denominational & Resource Statements of Faith on the Sovereignty of God

The Westminster Confession of Faith

"God, from all eternity, did, by the most wise and holy counsel of His own will, freely, and unchangeably ordain whatever comes to pass." [6] Here, seekers desiring to know who God is will trust that all of life is governed by His absolute immutability. In His sovereign rule, He possesses unchallengeable supreme wisdom.

Easton's Bible Dictionary defines God's sovereignty as His "absolute right to do all things according to His own good pleasure." [7]

Nave's Topical Bible lists well over 100 verses in the Christian Bible under the entry "sovereign". [8] All scripture is given to teach, inspire and to provide guidance for truths leading to salvation for eternal life as well as excellence in the quality of life for daily living.

The National Baptist Convention, USA, Inc. declares that as a Convention "We acknowledge the sovereignty of God by *What We Believe* as listed in our Articles of Faith Declaration of Belief." Note the context of Article IX of the Baptist Belief: [9]

Article IX. God's Purpose of Grace.

We believe the scriptures teach that election is the eternal purpose of God, according to which He graciously regenerates, sanctifies, and saves sinners;

that being perfectly consistent with the free agency of man, it comprehends all the means in connection with the end; that it is a most glorious display of God's sovereign goodness, being infinitely free, wise, holy, and unchangeable; that it utterly excludes boasting and promotes humility, love, prayer, praise, trust in God, and active imitation of His free mercy; that it encourages the use of means in the highest degree; that it may be ascertained by its effects in all who truly believe the Gospel; that it is the foundation of Christian assurance; and that to ascertain it with regard to ourselves demands and deserves the utmost diligence.

The Bethlehem Baptist Church has developed a statement on the sovereignty of God, which appears in the *Elder Affirmation of Faith*, to support a doctrine the elders of this church have given their heartfelt affirmation. Attached is what they affirm about God in Section 3 of their Statement of Faith. [10]

Section Three. Statement of Faith – God's Eternal Purpose and Election

3.1 We believe that God, from all eternity, in order to display the full extent of His glory for the eternal and ever-increasing enjoyment of all who love Him, did, by the most wise and holy counsel of His will, freely and unchangeably ordain and foreknow whatever comes to pass.

3.2 We believe that God upholds and governs all things - from galaxies to subatomic particles, from the forces of nature to the movements of nations, and from the public plans of politicians to the secret acts of solitary persons - all in accord with His eternal, all-wise purposes to glorify Himself, yet in such a way that He never sins, nor ever condemns a person unjustly; but that His ordaining and governing all things is compatible with the moral accountability of all persons created in His image.

3.3 We believe that God's election is an unconditional act of free grace which was given through His Son Christ Jesus before the world began. By this act God chose, before the foundation of the world, those who would be delivered from bondage to sin and brought to repentance and saving faith in His Son Christ Jesus.

God Is

The above messages provide spiritual breakthrough for countless numbers of Christian workers who seek solace in knowing and performing the perfectly divine will of God. God's sovereignty and the ability to know Him become a relentless pursuit as believers serve to bring glory to Him in the daily execution of their lives. Words become inadequate in the attempt to describe who God is and what is the majesty of His sovereignty, but scripture, one after the other tells who He is and the might of His power.

John 4:24 (ESV) –God is spirit, and those who worship Him must worship in spirit and truth.

1 John 4:8 (ESV) -Anyone who does not love does not know God, because God is love.

John 14:6 (ESV) –Jesus said to him, "I am the way, and the truth, and the life. No one comes to the Father except through Me.

Revelation 22:13 (ESV) - I am the Alpha and the Omega, the first and the last, the beginning and the end.

1 John 4:16 (ESV) - So we have come to know and to believe the love that God has for us. God is love, and whoever abides in love abides in God, and God abides in Him.

Deuteronomy 32:4 (ESV) - The Rock, His work is perfect, for all His ways are justice. A God of faithfulness and without iniquity, just and upright is He.

Exodus 3:14 (ESV) - God said to Moses, "I AM WHO I AM." And He said, "Say this to the people of Israel, 'I AM has sent me to you.'"

Titus 1:2 (ESV) - In hope of eternal life, which God, who never lies, promised before the ages began.

Luke 18:27 (ESV) - But He said, "What is impossible with men is possible with God.

Colossians 1:16 (ESV) - For by Him all things were created, in heaven and on earth, visible and invisible, whether thrones or dominions or rulers or authorities—all things were created through Him and for Him.

1 John 3:1-24 (ESV) - See what kind of love the Father has given to us, that we should be called children of God; and so we are. The reason why the world does not know us is that it did not know Him. Beloved, we are God's children now, and what we will be has not yet appeared; but we know that when He appears we shall be like Him, because we shall see Him as He is. And everyone who thus hopes in Him purifies himself as He is pure. Everyone who makes a practice of sinning also practices lawlessness; sin is lawlessness. You know that He appeared to take away sins, and in Him there is no sin.

Numbers 23:19 (ESV) - God is not man, that He should lie, or a son of man, that He should change His mind. Has He said, and will He not do it? Or has He spoken, and will He not fulfill it?

Deuteronomy 7:9 (ESV) - Know therefore that the LORD your God is God, the faithful God who keeps covenant and steadfast love with those who love Him and keep His commandments, to a thousand generations.

Genesis 1:1 (ESV) - In the beginning, God created the heavens and the earth.

Thoughts on Who God Is!

God is Love
God is Immutable
God is Majestic
God is Omnipotent
God is Omnipresent
God is Omniscient
God is Everlasting
God is Eternal
God is the Beginning and the End
God is our Redeemer
God is Shelter from the Storm
God is Always the Same: Yesterday, Today and Forever More
God is Hope for today and tomorrow
God is Our Everything
God is Merciful
God Forgives
God is Almighty
God is the Holy Spirit
God is Supreme
God is Divine
God is Holy
God is Mighty
God is Our Hope
God is Powerful
God Redeems
God is our Eternal Judge
God Reigns
God Delivers
God IS!

❖

CHAPTER TWO

The Mission of God for His Church

The Message of the Cross

Why is there a call for a continuous reliance and refocusing on the message "Where is Jesus the Christ, God's beloved Son in whom He is well pleased?" How valuable is this message to the people of God as they assume tasks of church management and leadership? Why am I purposefully structuring an entire volume of knowledge to directly connect church administration, management, and daily operations to the divine message of the cross at Calvary?

Why am I so passionate that leaders of the gospel remember that in all things, the mission of the church is the all-consuming message of redemption through Jesus at Calvary? Why am I insistent that administrators of ministries and individual organizers of assigned leadership tasks know and insist that as they serve, they remember Christ's resurrection from the grave? Why must this consciously convincing evidence be presented to proclaim adherence to the one mission for the church? Because *this is the work* of the church!

The church administration body of literature does not require another reference to *simply* outline the tenants of effective church organization. Rather, *HONOR to the Great Head of the Church* is written to provide a passionate theological perspective of the church's responsibility to place the message of the cross as the essential purpose for all operations of leadership and management conducted by the church.

Dr. William J. Shaw, past president of the National Baptist Convention, USA, INC., stated the idea well when he wrote "We must never forget who sent us and the specific task that the church was sent to perform in the world." [11] Dr. Shaw shared his views on God's intended mission for the church in an article, *The Heavenly Vision, the Mission of the Church*, Adult Study Guide, Sunday School Publishing Board. Dr. Shaw's national presidency was focused on serving a convention that operated from the message of a slogan he used throughout his tenure as president. The words of the slogan used in the convention were "Christ Only, Always." The undeniable objective of the President's motto was consistent with the message of his article. They both expressed that a reliance on the Lordship of Christ, and His redeeming message at the cross, are the only indicators that the church is operating in mission.

Without a doubt, the Lord's sacrifice at Calvary must remain front and central to every ministry, to all programmatic formats, and each service project in the church. This mindset is the representative indicator that quality church ministry exists. Such is the practice of a church in continued pursuit to seek Jesus Christ. The message of the cross carries with it an insistence for leaders to focus their assignments on works that symbolize for all to know why the church exists.

Our Obedience to Mature Discipleship

The Calvary message of redemption remains the guidepost for the church to mature in godliness. The *hill far away* is the symbol of relevance between man and his deliverance. An obligation to proclaim the gospel, to teach, and to witness with boldness and conviction becomes the mission of God's people in obedience to the sovereignty of God.

Every action that leads congregations to full participation in building up for kingdom living results from the church's pursuit to transform a membership from within a context of spiritual order and discipleship. *Each engagement becomes a relentless assignment to focus on God's Great Commission for the church.* That commission becomes a guiding light to grow in the grace and knowledge of Christ. It becomes the reference point for all engagements corresponding to maturity in spiritual formation and knowledge. Obedience to Matthew 28: 18-20 (KJV) provides readiness for believers to speak up, stand strong, and to ultimately live a life of commitment to our Savior's command to "go, reach, teach and then to go again."

The Christian hope calls for the children of God to enter into the realm of God, where the character of God infuses with all life and human relations to the core values of God's holy kingdom. [12]

When we begin to view all of life's commitments, those within and those outside the church, from the lens of the vision of a new heaven and a new earth, the assignments of life's daily journey are communicated from pure hearts, clean motives, and clarity of purpose. As followers of Jesus, we hold these views evident from our early experiences to our ending deeds from places of spiritual maturity. The process to obtain wisdom in Christian living follows having a determined mindset to obey and live a life pleasing to the will of the Father. It is a daily journey of sacrifice to self with a dependence on the one hope found only in God's Word. These actions lead to an upward climb of unity with Christ for service to Christ.

The Purposeful Church in Mission

Church mission used in the context of this book speaks of God's call to redeem lost man unto salvation and discipleship while participating in the great service of ministry organization. This single-minded, intentional, purposeful and repeated daily for a focus on Christ, leads learners to view organizational leadership and administration from its original context found in scripture. As a result, leadership theories and principles of management will always operate from within a theological framework honorable to edification that glorifies God in all church accomplishments.

On one continuum are the challenges of the church to perform day to day operations of leadership in administration. The ministries to manage human resources, to coordinate organizational objectives, direct operational procedures, and bring together ministry messages are all basic functions of church administration.

These variables of accomplishments are extremely important to designing the work of planning for growth within a system of procedures and guidelines. Their value to order is safeguarded by every definition of systematic structure imaginable; be it leadership expertise, administrative functioning, or organizational systems management. However, their worth, no matter how valuable, cannot replace all theological groundwork to maintain a Christ focused agenda for developing faithful discipleship within the total scope of church worthiness.

"That we may know Him, and the power of His resurrection, and the fellowship of His sufferings, being made conformable unto His death," (Philippians 3:10, KJV), is among scripture giants that articulate the message of the resurrection leading to the formation of power for the New Testament church.

The purpose for verse ten is the promised mission of God's covenant to redeem the lost back to him. It is in this intentional outcome that the church, God's people, will ultimately join in "conformity to the image of Christ." The will of God becomes the will of the church. As He commands, our hearts' desire is to reach perfection in Him. God's Word instructs the church to conduct its organizational responsibilities through a realization that structuring with effective human capital management is paramount to successful proclamation of its only mission. When He commands, the church conforms to His will. When He speaks, the church obeys.

How We May Know Him

Consider here how we will therefore align church leadership, administration, and systems organization from the preceding text (Philippians 3:10, KJV) to a commitment to join ministry with mission in support of "how we may know who we are" in Christ:

1. A church existing in maturity with scripture will "*know Him.*" The "*righteousness of God*" (Philippians 3:10, KJV) is the knowledge of Christ delivered through the preaching and teaching of anointed leaders who will rightly divide the Word, delivering for all listeners, sound biblical truths. Transformational leaders preach and teach with spiritual authority that leads to forgiveness of sin unto repentance from unrighteousness. Followers grow to operate in the fruit and gifts of the Holy Spirit that now resides within the hearts of the believers.

2. We may know him by "*The power of His resurrection* (Philippians 3:10, KJV)." This evidencing divine power fosters hope leading to *a church of power.* Believers become transformed by their faith into the image and likeness of Christ as they commune with him in daily meditation, consistent study and spiritual formation of prayer, fellowship, and discovery. Here effective church organization prepares members for powerful life changing education in worship, teaching, learning, training, and service.

3. We may know him by "*the fellowship of His sufferings* (Philippians 3:10, KJV)." Fellowship is friendship shared by common interests and

expectations. Fellowship in suffering is feeling the pain, distress, or problems of others. Suffering may even lead to pray as the Apostle Paul prayed when he acknowledged "Oh that I might know how to share Christ's pain and hurt." A church deeply committed to sharing with Christ in suffering partakes in the spiritual sufferings He endured on His way to the cross. The church suffers with unrepentant members and the sins of a lost world. The church suffers in the disobedience of loved ones with the obligations to deliver Christ to lost family members and love ones.

4. We are being *"made conformable unto His death"* (Philippians 3:10, KJV). This implies a gradual process of dying unto self daily. *"Likewise reckon ye also yourselves to be dead indeed unto sin, but alive unto God through Jesus Christ our Lord"* (Romans 6:11, KJV). The church that serves the call of the cross is engaged in acts of salvation unto good works. Deeds from the fruit of the vine signify that God's elect are being conformed to the image of His Son and are being fashioned unto His likeness. What is occurring now is the call to steadfast, immovable faith in Christ. Members grow in Christ like character with a lifelong calling to serve others.

As the church is converted to living out its mission from Christ and His calling to personal spiritual commitment, challenges are presented to the church to ask "how much are we committed to the mission of Jesus?" As the church decides on vision to devise yearly planning calendars for each new year of service, emphasis must be placed on a renewed commitment to living out God's command to faithful obedience to our Lord Jesus.

Dr. Elliott Cuff, past dean, current president, National Baptist Congress of Christian Education, National Baptist Convention, USA, Inc. wrote in the *Congress Study Guide* from a topic, *"Converting Mission Minded-less Churches to the Mission of Jesus Christ,"* to ask sound and thought provoking questions of today's church. [13]

The point of his inquiry was to insist that the church reflect continuously on its heavenly mission. He compared the mission of God to everyday practices found in the context of works from this generation of churchgoers.

From Dr. Cuff's critique, it appears that traditions and rituals are important to the work; but insisted that the church must give active thought to how much emphasis is sincerely being placed on God's grand mission. The most important mission for the church is to live a faithful life, one in pursuit of serving Christ. These thoughts are certainly points of impact necessary to spiritual growth for all believers.

In reflecting on the focus presented here, the gospel message is therefore significant to believers' transformation. The mission of the church is not to become an attraction in the world as such, but to attract the world to the kingdom of God. The resurrection power of Jesus transforms followers into disciples who become powerful to the kingdom. Jesus desires the church to remain His ambassadors for every generation, without ceasing until He returns. How the church affects the Christian message to remain constant in the midst of the many challenges of the time is a question the church continues to answer.

CHAPTER THREE

❖

The Church and God's Mission

Apostolic Teachings from the Early Church

A question has been asked of today's church, "How did we get here?" How did the church move away from the apostles' teachings found in the Early New Testament Church? A term used to express the supreme authority for the teachings of Jesus Christ has been identified as *Sola Scriptura*, meaning the sufficiency of scripture. *Sola Scriptura* is of itself, a simple phase. Its meaning is that scripture alone is the Lord's authority for the church. The value for scripture only, emphasizes that the unadulterated Word of God is complete for all to obtain its purpose and receive its message. When God revealed His will to men inspired to write, scripture became the supreme authority of God for all to read, to hear, to live, and to believe unto the fullness of faith. During the sixteenth-century Reformation movements, *Sola Scriptura*, the Bible alone, was the all-sufficient way to discover salvation and the continued pursuit to a deeper life in Christ.

Prior to the biblical teachings of the Reformation, Catholic church theologians had previously promoted that *reason* (logic and debate), *leadership* (bishops' interpretations) and *rituals* (beliefs and traditions not found in scripture), were the true interpreters of scripture. That kind of thinking had placed the teaching authority of the bishops over scripture itself. But *Sola Scriptura* had meant that the Bible alone is the only infallible Word of God.[14] For believers, the Bible as the infallible Word of truth and divine light is indeed the supreme authority over the church.

Reformation efforts took on aggressive responsibilities to restore to the church the *simple principles* of the teachings taught by the apostles in the Early Church days. The Early Church believed that all doctrine must be proven from scripture. What had initially been taught by way of oral instruction had now become written scripture. The written text, the Bible, God's Holy Word, is now God's special revelation and His message to the church. Thusly, the Bible is God's inspired Word and the ultimate authority for the church. [15]

The principle of scripture as the sufficiency of supreme authority carries in it truths that are clear and simple.[16] The clarity of scripture means that in scripture, persons read them to discover salvation for eternal life. Pastors and teachers are necessary to help bring understanding to the message of salvation (Ephesians 4:11-12, KJV). They are essential to teaching believers how to live in faith, how to discover peace, and the basics to finding joy in living out the hope of the risen Christ. Bible truths are certain. They speak as the authority of God's grand mission for the church, which is honor to *Christ*. Scripture is therefore the perfect and only standard of spiritual truth.

From this regard, theologians such as William Tyndale[17] felt strongly that the Bible was intended to respond to the needs of all regardless of status or creed, that understanding God was meant to include, *"even the ploughboy,"* in the learning of scripture. From that philosophical stance to this day, great efforts have been made to translate the Bible into many common languages.[18] Throughout this text, several versions of the original Book are used to indicate this author's affinity to insert a favored version in places where it is judged that clarity of thought comes through the reading of that particular translation.

To summarize, there are three critical themes true to the basic message of Sola Scriptura. The themes are: The Bible is the supreme authority. The Bible is sufficient. The Bible is clear. [19] It stands to reason that God desires for the Word to be made plain for all to understand and live by its interpretations and its messages.

Study in scripture opens blinded eyes and awakens readers to believe that justification in righteousness is found in God's amazing grace. All of scripture gives us grace for faith in Jesus Christ, and Christ alone. Teaching the grace of God's holy Word sustains hope with a continuous trust in the supreme authority of God.

A Singular Focus: Spiritual Maturity in Christ

In their book, *Simple Church*, Tom Rainer and Eric Geiger [20] shared mission principles churches can use to return to the Lord's mandates and His process for teaching, leading, making, and keeping disciples. They highlighted that church leaders should operate around the simple definition of administering with the results being *spiritual transformation of the believer.* Teaching to promote spiritual transformation is paired with strategies in implementations for personal and congregational growth. Organizational methods are the gateway to produce viable strategies that develop members through the stages toward spiritual maturity within the congregation.[21]

The process for church administration, church management, and all levels of leadership is basic to concepts that create environments to move all systems in management toward increased spiritual formation for members. All design elements are centered on the target goal. Design is the process to develop and grow disciples in the way of the gospel. This targeted focus is continuously communicated and is intentional in delivery. The outcome is to mature and transform membership for faithful worship and service. As a direct result, the kingdom of God is nurtured in sound doctrinal teaching and preaching. Members move unerringly toward growth in steadfast love and hope as they experience the power of God moving in their lives and at work in the lives of others within the congregation.

This outcome to grow in the knowledge of Christ, to attract membership and community to the qualities and personality of Christ is the byproduct of the strategy, which is *the process.* There should however, be no confusion between process and outcome. Leadership meets membership at the place where people exist in their relationship with Christ and with their fellowman. *Spiritual growth is the progression of results achieved from the works of labor in both management and leadership.* This is administration in the hands of qualified and capable leaders to advance the church closer to its singular purpose with a sense that, in time, they will grow to arrive at the desired outcomes.

The sufficiency of scripture paired with the mandates of organizational integrity is the partnership God uses to move the church, His people, through the stages of spiritual growth and maturity to accomplish the *work of the church.* Programs and church initiatives must be clearly communicated throughout the congregation that they are necessary to the operation of growth in faith. Spiritual platforms of this style move members through the many stages of church life necessary for regeneration, sanctification and on to transformation.

To accomplish these mandates, scripture, effective leadership, spiritual formation, and devoted memberships pair with the theoretical foundations of management to deliver Christ to all who would hear and follow. This spiritual synergy becomes the perspectives vital to leadership and organizational administration. [22]

As guardians of His mission, we, the church of God, are expected to administrate His plans by demonstrating the values of the kingdom Jesus taught and lived. How does the church operate in managing the affairs of the Master within the congregation while keeping a constant focus on biblical regeneration leading to maturity? Growth in spiritual matters from persons operating in their spiritual gifts is an indicator of maturity in the Lord. Being guided by the Spirit to live the abundant life in Christ is another quality indictor of maturity in Christ.

The next three sections of the book will present new perspectives to address a paradigm shift for moving the church on to a transformational model of teaching, serving, and leading. From administrative theory to daily practices in leadership and organizational management, all essential to advancing a kingdom mindset, Sections Two, Three, and Four serve to guide expansive growth for the twenty-first century church. With a call to transitioning the need for God's people to operate in His singular mission, clear and convincing evidence from this volume of study, supported continuously by scripture, should bring this clarion focus to new light.

Transforming the church to serve the fullness of Christ through the operational roles of leaders, managers, and administrators is a relatively new concept. The desire is that the church will submit to the mission of the Good News Message of Christ in every ministry or operational endeavor, for all to honor and to obey His holy will.

SECTION TWO

A Transformational Model in Leadership

❖

CHAPTER FOUR

Spiritual Authority in the Church

A study of the spiritual authority God gave to the church is valuable to respecting, and most importantly, to honoring the message of Headship for all ministry commissions in the church.

Christ, Chief Cornerstone and Head of the Church

A cornerstone is described as the architectural foundation for a building. The cornerstone is the first stone laid and is set as a reference standard for all other stones. Its purpose is to strengthen and sustain all subsequent construction of the eventual structure. Historically, this initial building block was basic to how the building's framework would conform to all angles and to the overall dimensions of the cornerstone. Upon securing the cornerstone and setting its range in position, the remaining portions of the building would be constructed to the consistency of the initial foundation, the cornerstone, the base support of the total structure.

As the first stone set in the construction, a cornerstone determines the size, scope and dimension of the entire structure. From this perspective, serving as a powerful position marker, cornerstones are indicators of the overall integrity of the building. In other words, the building will not be able to stand against the removal of the cornerstone.

Old (Isa 28:16; Zech 10:4, KJV) and New (Eph 2:20; 1Peter 2:6-7, KJV) Testament scripture(s) speak of Jesus Christ as the Chief Foundation and Glorious Cornerstone in the construction of the Church. The Prophet Isaiah wrote in Isaiah 28:16, (ESV), saying, "Behold, I am the one who has laid as a foundation in Zion, a stone, a tested stone, a precious cornerstone, of a sure foundation. Psalm 118:22, (ESV), speaks of the Messiah, stating, "The stone that the builders rejected has become the cornerstone."

Another significant text from the teaching of the Apostle Paul, also points to Jesus as the Cornerstone, "So then you are no longer strangers and aliens, but you are fellow citizens with the saints and members of the household of God, built on the foundation of the Apostles and prophets, Christ Jesus himself being the cornerstone" (Ph 2:19-20, ESV).

The alignment that connects construction and building to the purpose and coming of Jesus, first as the Messiah and secondly as the Chief Cornerstone is symbolic to acknowledging Christ's position as the Great Head of the Church. God provided a pathway that the church of Christ would be built sequentially on the foundation foretold from the prophets, and on to the teachings of the apostles.

At the time of the writings of the New Testament, the founding of the church was still in its early years. Contention was as present, as was growth throughout the church world during that time. Disputations developed as members of the church were prone in those days, similar to the way members are today, to drifting away from the knowledge of true doctrine.

Warnings found in Galatians 1:8-9 (ESV) were given so the church would maintain obedience to the truth of God and to avoid seeking the favor of man. Following His three-year preparation in study and with the aid and comfort of the Holy Spirit, the Apostle Paul journeyed to Jerusalem. His purpose was to make known to the disciples that he had prepared himself and thusly was also a fellow apostle. His obligation and commitment to the truth of the gospel were in agreement with the knowledge of the Lord as presented by Apostles Peter (Cephas), James, and John (Galatians 2:9, ESV). Paul taught and preached the same gospel as Christ's apostles. Paul had been delivered from persecuting saints to one who was a follower and teacher on behalf of the Good News Savior. He therefore taught that believing in Jesus Christ was foundational to the faith.

Jesus is the "Chief Cornerstone" because He was the standard laid to deliver revelations of truth; truth from the time of the apostles to teachings for the church today. Therefore, Jesus Christ is the foundation of the church. All who believe the truths of these teachings become "fellow citizens with the saints and members of the household of God" (Ephesians 2:19, ESV).

God's Word is His ultimate guide to teach to all who believe that Jesus is the Chief Cornerstone; the Great Head of His Church. The following scriptural references are provided to describe Christ as the Cornerstone of our faith, as well as the Head of the church. Carefully study each scripture reference below to embrace and believe in this doctrinal truth.

Scripture References for Christ as Head of the Church[23]

Psalm 118:22 (NKJV). The stone which the builders rejected has become the chief cornerstone.

Ephesians 1:22 (ESV). And He put all things under His feet, and gave Him as head over all things to the church.

Ephesians 4:12 (NASB). For the equipping of the saints for the work of service, to the building up of the body of Christ.

Ephesians 5:23 (NASB). For the husband is the head of the wife, as Christ also is the head of the church, He Himself being the Savior of the body.

1 Corinthians 11:3 NASB). But I want you to understand that Christ is the head of every man, and the man is the head of a woman, and God is the head of Christ.

Colossians 1:18 (NASB). He is also head of the body, the church; and He is the beginning, the firstborn from the dead, so that He Himself will come to have first place in everything.

Colossians 2:10 (NASB). And in Him you have been made complete, and He is the head over all rule and authority.

Scripture References to Know Christ as Head of the Church[24]
Christ, the head of the church has pre-eminence in all things.

Colossians 1:18 (NASB) He is also head of the body, the church; and He is the beginning, the firstborn from the dead, so that He Himself will come to have first place in everything.

Ephesians 1:22 (NASB) And He put all things in subjection under His feet, and gave Him as head over all things to the church.

1 Corinthians 11:3 (NASB) But I want you to understand that Christ is the head of every man, and the man is the head of a woman, and God is the head of Christ.

Christ's Fullness is His Authority

Colossians 1:8 (NASB) declares that Christ is the Head of the body and the church is born from His deity. As the Head of the church, Christ is the image of God, the visible form of God's invisibility. *As the fountain of authority, everything in the church flows from His power and His authority.* The glory of God's redemptive plan is upheld by Christ, "who is the beginning and the end of all things." All matters of the church emanate from Christ. His pre-eminence from glory to everlasting glory grants Him power, rank, and authority over the entire universe, inclusive of the church.

Christ is the mind of the church; His headship with creation grants that all things were created by Him and for Him. He was present with God in creation. In the beginning, all things that were made were created by Him, as He is the first born of all things in creation. Colossians 1:15, (ESV) proclaims that "He is the image and embodiment of God; He is the firstborn of all things." All leadership, all ministry, and all works of grace are therefore, under His Lordship. Man's ideas for the church are meaningless, unless they emanate from the heart and message of Christ.

In an article entitled *"Who Is the Head of the Church?"* author Bill Elliff[25] challenged church leaders to consider who is in charge and dare to ask why it made a difference.

Point by point, this author, highlighted a provocative treaty on behalf of our risen Savior as the Lord and Headship of the church. His message leaves the readers with understanding for our Lord and why He reigns supreme in this life as God's appointed Savior and therefore Head of His elect. [26]

Churches, whose leader's function in the power and might of the Lord, will bear witness for all to know that the entirety of God's authority is aimed toward the cross at Calvary. These leaders teach that a place called Calvary is where God gave His body, whole and blameless, without reproach for the sins of all. These leaders teach Jesus Christ, crucified, yet redeemed. The expectation is that others will come to know the glory of the Lord that reigns over all and through all. The result is that the church receives the glad news to obediently submit to His Lordship.

Jesus is the Rock of salvation. Christ's love is a shield. He is Alpha and Omega, the beginning and the end. He is matchless in His essence and His deity. There is absolutely none to compare with Him. God "put all things under His feet and gave Him as head over all things to the church, which is His body" (Ephesians 1:22-23, ESV).

The church, the called out, the very elect of God's holiness was formed so that salvation in Christ would be manifested to complete its regeneration and to offer redemption. It therefore pleased God to allow everything to advance through Him and in Him. As the Great Head of the church, all honor and obedience are due Christ. He is justified and He justifies. He gave His life as ransom for the sins of fallen humanity that lost man may be redeemed from death and burial to an everlasting eternal rebirth. This is the *Act of Christ on behalf of the church*. His death at Calvary and resurrection from the grave burst open to establish and affirm for all who would believe that He is the Great I Am; all to Him is owed.

The Spirit of Christ lives in every believer to will and to do that which pleases the Lord. He is help in times of trouble. He is refuge from the storms of life. He guides footsteps and sets believers free to stand firm in the faith. His leadership initiates submitted followship. Therefore, where the Spirit leads, the faithful follows. Regardless of the multiplicity of messaging in doctrinal truths, Christ is the deliverer for the Church. The glorious truth is that Christ is in fact, God, the creator and sustainer of all things. His authority for the church is full and complete.

Spiritual Authority: God's Method of Divine Leadership

Ephesians 5:22–25 (KJV) tells of the divinely ordained relationship between a husband and his wife. This teaching of order in the universe for marriage is the covenant union between a man and a woman. The text also gives value to believers for understanding the teachings of Jesus as the Head of the church.

"Wives, submit yourselves to your own husbands as you do to the Lord. For the husband is the head of the wife in the same way that Christ is the head of the church, His body, of which He is the Savior. Now as the church submits to Christ, so also wives should submit to their husbands in everything. Husbands, love your wives, just as Christ loved the church and gave himself up for her."

The passage teaches that wives are to submit to the sufficiency of their husbands as the church is to submit to the all sufficiency of Christ. Husbands sacrificially love their wives just as Christ's love led Him to die for the church. In this context, Jesus is called the "Head of the church which is His body." He is also the Savior of the body. Husbands are likewise saviors for their wives.

God's authority has been given that man would receive power to live the laws of His Word. Obedience to the law gives grace to embrace truths to govern lives in submission to its messages. This power in deliverance is available to every believer. Understanding the authority of God is the first order of respecting and following leadership. The authority of all things spiritual, from God's privileges and gifts, provides that we grasp all He has made available to reach the greatest potential in Him. Spiritual power is released so believers may grow through acts of repentance and submission.

When the church operates in obedience to the spiritual authority of God, leaders and members experience opportunity to accomplish His purpose in the duties assigned to the church. In the functions of duty for obedience to the Lordship of Christ, an atmosphere of influence evolves from a genuine connectedness to the Holy Spirit. Christians are heirs of God and joint-heirs with Christ (Romans 8:1, KJV) with full access to the Father by His Holy Spirit (Ephesians 2:18, KJV). The abundant life is therefore experienced as a result of the relationship between God and His people.

This established authority starts and ends with Christ. Church leaders have been given positions of authority to honor Christ by submitting their roles of authority to His law. Their dedication to call is to obtain wisdom for growth in service to others (Ephesians 4:11-13, KJV). Pastors, elders and bishops submit to the authority of God to teach, supervise and "watch over the souls" of their members (Hebrews 13:17, KJV). These leaders are held to a greater accountability to God (James 3:1, KJV); and their members acknowledge and submit to those who cover them in things relating to spiritual matters (1 Thessalonians 5:12-13, KJV). The aforementioned are a few of the examples of the church operating in unity with one another before God and all who profess a faith in Him. As a result of all parts submitting to the order of God, the church is strengthened to endure and carry out its divine mission in the world.

Defining Spiritual Leadership Authority

What is Spiritual Leadership?

"The effectiveness of your work will never rise above your ability to lead and influence others." According to John Maxwell, of the many significant terms used to define leadership, there is one factor that runs throughout all definitions; that word is influence: the ability to stimulate others to have some kind of effect on their thinking, their belief, or their conduct. In this regard, for John Maxwell, leadership is influence! [27]

Kruse gives a definition for leadership as a process of social influence, which maximizes the efforts of others, towards the achievement of a goal. [28]

Here are several single sentence definitions for defining leadership from persons respected in the field of leadership development throughout the literature.

- Peter Drucker: "The definition of a leader is someone who has followers." [29]
- Warren Bennis: "Leadership is the capacity to translate vision into reality."[30]
- Bill Gates: "As we look ahead into the next century, leaders will be those who empower others."[31]
- John Maxwell: "Leadership is influence - nothing more, nothing less."[32]

A closer definition for leadership in relation to ministry is one offered by Bill Lawrence. He writes that "leadership is the act of influencing and serving others out of Christ's interests in their lives so that they accomplish God's purposes for and through them." [33]

Christian leadership is not rooted in worldly notions of success, such as the love of money or the attainment of power; and maybe not necessarily the single notion of influence. Influence is however, valuable to connecting the message of Christ to the world that persons who are lost in sin may know Him and be saved. Leading from a place that embodies the spiritual authority of the Lord is leading that presents Jesus, Christ of light, to a dark world. Our Lord taught on the importance of leading to serve others. He spoke against gaining the whole word and losing one's own righteousness. The idea of leading for the sake of self gain was looked upon and expressed negatively by the Lord when he taught on the importance of leading on behalf of others.

Spiritual leadership authority occurs when godly leaders embrace vision for the continued hope of renewal in Christ for the church. Leaders are called upon to possess a strong sense of authority in conviction and resolution. They have to take chances others may normally decide to ignore. Leaders are consumed with the direction the church will take in matters large and small. Daily, they sort through questions for the advancement and the hope of a congregation.

When problems arise, spiritual leaders must follow the authority of scripture, biblical teaching, training, and the sage counsel of others knowledgeable and experienced in ministry leadership. Operating in wisdom of this quality is support for members to move closer to the mandates and will of God. The vision to stay on Christ's message of redemption with a focused commitment to remain grounded and faithful to purpose becomes the clarion call for leaders who effectively operate under the spiritual authority of the Head for the church.

An appropriate summary for this section comes as a plea to the leadership of local assemblies to insist that members submit to the Lordship of Christ. As Christ loved the church, leaders and all church members obey and submit to Him. Psalms 84:11 (KJV) reminds us that "the Lord God is a sun and shield; that the Lord gives grace and glory; that no good thing will He withhold from them that walk uprightly." Psalms 91:4 (KJV) also alerts the church to knowing that "God's truths will be as a shield and buckler." His divine protection serves as an armor of defense against all blows of life that can be thrown toward a godly leader.

Submitting to God and standing firm in the strength of His authority for any leader yields a character and disposition closely aligned to the mind and thusly, the works of Christ. The Lord of all things will provide for all needs. He is the sustainer of every hope. He will honor His Word to deliver for every need.

Bible Examples in Leadership

A study of leaders from the Bible presents a wide range of personalities in leadership abilities and leadership styles. Author, Brooks Faulker, Lifeway Corporation, wrote to highlight seven leaders whose works played significant roles in advancing a theological view, as well as a theoretical framework of leadership models for the church. The seven leaders presented were described in an article entitled *"Seven biblical models of leadership."*[34] Faulkner described the leaders by relating the accomplishments of each leader to his character and skills. The impact they had on their followers and the lasting influence of their deeds and conduct with the people they led is significant to a study of their leadership styles. The effect they had on others and the results of their leading serve to add to present day literature for teaching personal and organizational leadership development.

These leaders, inclusive of the Apostle Paul, Joshua, Barnabas, Nehemiah, Moses, Elijah, and Peter, were characters who were more than persons from biblical history, individuals merely contributing to Bible knowledge. Rather, each leader played a major role in representing part of God's grand design for how powerful leaders can affect their followers.

Throughout the Bible, other righteous leaders and also those counted as faithless leaders of wickedness and doubt, can be researched to supply the church with examples of these leaders' strengths and weaknesses. Leaders, both men, along with some women, who behaved righteously or who practiced evil in the sight of God and man, give the church deeper insight into each character's leadership style. Studies in biblical leadership are powerful tools for the church to pursue throughout the year. Having this required knowledge in biblical leadership styles serves to help impact a church when choosing persons to deliver the message of Christ, as well as persons to serve in leadership in the congregation.

❖

The Pastor: God's Agent as Church Leader

Obey your leaders and submit to them, for they keep watch over your souls as those who will give an account. Let them do this with joy and not with grief, for this would be unprofitable for you. (Hebrews 13:17, NASB)

Pastoral Leadership Authority

Chapter Five is undoubtedly one of the most valuable sections in the book. Pastors, God's established agents for church leadership, serve to function in the office of pastoral spiritual authority for the church. God gave pastors of local assemblies the responsibilities to care for and to provide for the overall spiritual welfare of members. Pastors shepherd, lead, preach, teach, guide, and mentor the example of Christ's love to those in their care. The authority of the pastor to bring lost individuals to a saving and full relationship with the Lord is an awesome task; one necessitated by God in His Word.

A friend and mentor in scripture, a pastor and an author in Christian education leadership, Dr. Geoffrey V. Guns wrote in a splendid work, *Understanding Spiritual Leadership Authority: A Practical and Biblical Model for Today's Church Leaders,* that God "has established pastoral spiritual leaders and has set them over His church for the express purpose of leading His people" (Numbers 27:12-23, KJV).35 Pastors lead and direct the ministry, mission, worship, teaching, preaching, and administrative affairs of the church.

In a work entitled *Biblical Eldership* by writer Alexander Strauch, [36] there are major responsibilities given to define the role of a pastor. He highlights three categories as those of preacher/teacher, leader/administrator, and shepherd/overseer.

The pastor is first an elder. With the support of lay leaders in the church, the pastor is responsible for the following: 1) oversee the church (1 Timothy 3:12, KJV); 2) rule over the church (1 Timothy 5:17, KJV); 3) feed the church (1 Peter 5:2, KJV); and 4) guard the doctrine of the church (Titus 1:9, KJV).

Scripture Passages on Pastoral Leadership[37]

The following passages of scripture bring light to understanding the role and responsibilities of a pastor:

> 1 Peter 5:3, (KJV) contains a wonderful description of a balanced pastoral ministry: "Neither as being lords over God's heritage, but being examples to the flock."

> The pastor's authority is not something to be "lorded over" on the church; rather, a pastor is to be an example of truth, love, and godliness for God's flock to follow. (Matthew 20:25-25, NKJV)

> A pastor is "the steward of God" (Titus 1:7, ESV), and he is answerable to God for his leadership in the church."

> Hebrews 13:17 – (ESV) Obey your leaders and submit to them, for they are keeping watch over your souls, as those who will have to give an account. Let them do this with joy and not with groaning, for that would be of no advantage to you.

> Acts 20:28 – (ESV) Pay careful attention to yourselves and to all the flock, in which the Holy Spirit has made you overseers, to care for the church of God, which he obtained with His own blood.

1 Timothy 3:2 – (ESV) Therefore an overseer must be above reproach, the husband of one wife, sober-minded, self-controlled, respectable, hospitable, able to teach.

Titus 1:6 - (ESV) If anyone is above reproach, the husband of one wife, and his children are believers and not open to the charge of debauchery or insubordination.

1 Timothy 3:1-7 – (ESV) The saying is trustworthy: If anyone aspires to the office of overseer, he desires a noble task. Therefore an overseer must be above reproach, the husband of one wife, sober-minded, self-controlled, respectable, hospitable, able to teach, not a drunkard, not violent but gentle, not quarrelsome, not a lover of money. He must manage his own household well, with all dignity keeping his children submissive, for if someone does not know how to manage his own household, how will he care for God's church?

Titus 1:5-9 - (ESV) This is why I left you in Crete, so that you might put what remained into order, and appoint elders in every town as I directed you— if anyone is above reproach, the husband of one wife, and his children are believers and not open to the charge of debauchery or insubordination. For an overseer, as God's steward, must be above reproach. He must not be arrogant or quick-tempered or a drunkard or violent or greedy for gain, but hospitable, a lover of good, self-controlled, upright, holy, and disciplined. He must hold firm to the trustworthy word as taught, so that he may be able to give instruction in sound doctrine and also to rebuke those who contradict it.

Titus 1:9 – (ESV) He must hold firm to the trustworthy word as taught, so that he may be able to give instruction in sound doctrine and also to rebuke those who contradict it.

1 Timothy 5:17 – (ESV) Let the elders who rule well be considered worthy of double honor, especially those who labor in preaching and teaching.

Seven Pastors Contribute to Chapter Five

Because pastors have been commissioned by God to watch over the souls of those in their charge, they are held accountable for accomplishments and problems found in the ministry. This is a huge responsibility; one that must not to be taken lightly. Surely this obligation weighs heavily on the hearts of pastors daily. It is an absolute necessity that a congregation is confident that their leaders take pleasure in what they do. Members enjoy thinking that their pastors care about their spiritual wellbeing and also think of them as family and friends. Although congregants may not equate benefits from a pastor from a material advantage, they desire to see and experience spiritual warmth and even uplift from observing the joy their pastors take in leading, advising, and teaching in the assembly.

While I am eternally filled with gratitude for the leading of the Holy Spirit to pursue and complete this study to Honor our heavenly Father through His Son Jesus as the Great Shepherd and Head of the church, I acknowledge that I have not been called to the office of pastor. As such, I will not count myself as an authority with authentic experiences in that office. After seeking spiritual guidance to effectively present the work of a pastor in this volume of study, I felt led to ask pastors to give assistance to the writing of Chapter Five. I, therefore, sought pastors from within the Arkansas church conventions to assist with the process.

The procedure to include pastors as contributors to the book began with a *Letter of Consent to Participate* with signature and check off boxes to agree or not to agree to participate in the questionnaire. A total of ten pastors were invited to complete an eight-question survey with a final count of seven successfully returning their written or verbal responses. Each pastor's *Informed Consent* was returned to confirm his participation in the survey.

Four of the seven pastors returned written responses and three pastors dictated their answers via recordings. I wrote and edited each of the three oral responses. The following letter, consent form, and the actual questionnaire of the eight questions asked is included in this section. The following pages will present each pastor's answers to the questions. I am forever grateful to these pastors who took time from their busy schedules to support this project. I sincerely pray that God blesses them continually.

The Informed Consent Letter Sent to Each Pastor[38]

Dear Pastor _____

I would like your help and participation with Chapter Five of a book I am presently writing: _HONOR to the Great Head of the Church: A Transformational Model for Church Leadership, Administration, and Management_. Chapter Five is entitled "The Pastor: God's Agent for Church Leadership."

While the literature, including God's holy Word, is filled with serious discussions and volumes of research detailing the role and perspectives of a pastor in a church, I desire to give fresh authenticity to this chapter beyond my attempt to present and discuss what is gathered from data and even biblical interpretation. Clearly, I am not a pastor.

I have therefore chosen seven pastors from the community and state convention works to be included in this present volume of study. If you decide to participate in the writing of this book I will be more than pleased to include your responses within the Chapter Five discussion.

I have composed a total of eight questions for you to provide answers to from within a five sentence limit for each question. If you need more space to give adequate attention to your details, I will work with up to six or seven concise statements for those questions that may require more elaboration. Please sir, carefully utilize your most concisely worded language in order to save space. Thank you!

Please read the following Consent to Participate and to Include My Writings information paragraphs carefully. If you do not wish to take part, return this form with your signature at the appropriate boxed category. However, if you are interested in taking part, please give your answer to each question asked. Your answers will be presented in the final draft of the book just as you provide it in your return email. Only minor adjustments to any required editing may be considered. Your work will not be paraphrased or summarized.

You will have considerable time to respond back with your answers. I am working to complete the book by the first of February. For further information you may call me at 870-489-6462.

Thank you for your help. I am so pleased to include your responses in the book.

Yours sincerely,
Margarette W. Williams

The Statement of Consent for Signature

Consent to Participate and to Include My Writings in Chapter Five. Confidentiality Factors.

I agree □ to participate
I do not agree □ to participate
in the writing of your book _HONOR To The Great Head of the Church: A Transformational Model for Church Leadership, Administration, and Management_. Any information collected during the course of the study will be maintained on a confidential basis and access will be restricted to this person conducting the writings and individual editors of the book until its publication. Your name and church employment will be disclosed in the chapter with the answers you provided to this researcher. With your permission and your returned answers, I will proceed to add your responses to this Volume One book of the Transformational Church Administration Series.

_____ Date _____
Pastor's Name

Church Name _____
Church Address _____

The Eight Questionnaire Survey[39]

The Pastor: God's Agent for Church Leadership

1. Please give your philosophy to biblical visionary leadership as it relates to God's mission and purpose for the church.

2. Express your understanding of spiritual authority for the church. Will you share your thoughts on spiritual leadership authority?

3. Share your thoughts on two interrelated models of leadership styles: transformational leadership and servant leadership. Which one has more value for you as a church pastor? Would you say that you are more likely to embrace one style over the other? Why or why not?

4. What is the pastor's role in church administration?

5. What does this statement mean for you and your congregation: "The pastor serves as change agent?"

6. Provide expression for this thought, "The cost of leadership."

7. What are competences & essential qualities for effective pastoral leadership?

8. Your thoughts on a pastor's personal life and the impact on the life and health of a congregation.

Pastoral Responses from Survey Questionnaire

Pastor Glenn Barnes, Pine Hill Missionary Baptist Church, Pine Bluff, AR

Please give your philosophy to biblical visionary leadership as it relates to God's mission and purpose for the church.

My philosophy for the church is rooted in the Old Testament. Malachi 1:11, (NASB) reads "for from the rising of the sun even to its setting, My name will be great among the nations, and in every place incense is going to be offered to My name, and a grain offering that is pure; for My name will be great among the nations," says the LORD of hosts." The text gives the purpose for God's calling of Israel and for choosing her. She was His agent of revelation to the world. The church is God's agent of revelation to the world today. The church has the responsibility to use everything God has given her to win the world to Himself. Spiritual leadership as it relates to God' mission and purpose, is based on the end goal and not on anything else. The focus is on God's redeeming hope and what comes at the end; leading the world to Christ.

Express your understanding of spiritual authority of the church. Will you share your thoughts on spiritual leadership authority?

When I think of spiritual authority, I find many examples in the Old Testament. Moses was the leader of the children of Israel; however, God used others to do specific things under the leadership of Moses. God gives authority to the man that He wants to lead. Authority is the God commanded power for the assignment. Leadership authority is the power, therefore the authority, to lead with success and to be effective.

Share your thoughts on two interrelated models of leadership styles in the church: transformational leadership and servant leadership. Which one has, if any, more value for you as a church pastor? Would you state that you are more likely to embrace one style over the other? Why or why not?

I believe I embrace servant leadership. Yes, I would consider myself a servant leader. However, there are times when elements of transformational leadership are essential and must be used. For example, I believe the size of a church can determine the need to embrace levels of transformational leadership. Large churches must depend on training leaders to support the leadership with skills necessary for effective management. It would be impossible to reach everyone without transformational leaders supporting the vision. That paradigm is most effective if you need to place members into groups for organization.

What is the pastor's role in church administration?

The pastor's role in church administration is to organize, train, and hold members accountable. I believe direction that sets changes in administration should be determined by the pastor.

What does this statement mean for you and your congregation: "The pastor serves as change agent?"

I believe the Pastor should initiate and manage change. He should serve as the principle change agent in the church.

Provide expression for this thought, "The cost of leadership."

According to 1st Timothy 4:15 (NIV) – "Be diligent in these matters; give yourself wholly to them, so that everyone may see your progress; and 2nd Timothy 2:3-4 (KJV) - "Thou therefore endure hardness, as a good soldier of Jesus Christ. No man that warreth entangleth himself with the affairs of this life; that he may please him who hath chosen him to be a soldier." The cost spoken of here is that the pastor must give himself completely to ministry. Leaders must be intentional in everything they do. They must give themselves to the cause of ministry. As with the cost associated with other professions, pastoral ministry is a lifetime commitment. It is difficult to measure the sacrifice of the Apostle Paul and His example of suffering for the call to ministry that was placed upon His life.

What do you determine to be some competences and essential qualities for effective pastoral leadership?

A significant scripture comes to mind as I think of pastoral leadership. Found in 1Timothy 3: 1-7 are three primary categories describing the role of leadership. These areas point to the pastor as a student of scripture, a man of faith, and a man of payer.

Your thoughts on a pastor's personal life and the impact it has on the life and health of a congregation:

The Pastor should keep his personal life in order. We all are human and have the propensity to make mistakes but we must "bring our bodies under subjection, lest after we preached to others, we end up being a castaway" (1st Corinthians 9:27, (KJV). Sin can sabotage any life.

Pastor Brian Castle, Indiana Street Missionary Baptist Church, Pine Bluff

Please give your philosophy to biblical visionary leadership as it relates to God's mission and purpose for the church

Biblical visionary leadership as it relates to God's mission and purpose for the church is the primary vehicle which moves God's people from their current position (station) to the realities of the manifest promises and purposes of God. The Biblical record reveals spirit-led visionary leadership submitted to the call of God (His Word) which moves God's people from where they are too literal places they have never walked before. Biblical visionary leadership moves God's people beyond the status quo into the eternal possibilities of life in the presence of an almighty God.

Let the Biblical record speak; Noah leads his family into the Ark trusting the call of God (His Word) to arrive at a new day and a new place he has not been before (Genesis 6:9 – 9:17). Abraham answered the call of "visionary leadership" to be led to a land God would show him (Genesis 12:1). Moses answers the call of "visionary leadership" (the Exodus testimony) to lead the people of God out of Egypt to a "place of promise" they have never dwelled in before (Exodus 3:1-6). Not only does the "visionary leadership" of Moses move God's people physically, but spiritually they are transformed from a "people" into a "nation," from a "crowd" into a "worshipping congregation" something they have never been before. I could continue with this list, but I will close out here "with a summation based on the life and work of our Lord and Savior, Jesus Christ. Jesus' call and visionary leadership exemplified through His presence, preaching and teaching, not only announced the breakthrough of the kingdom of God into the present age, but the reality of how men might be transformed by the "new birth" to become citizens and heirs of the kingdom of God; places men desired to be, but had not been before! Therefore, the implication is simple; the church of God should still have leadership answering the call of Biblical "visionary leadership" to move God's people beyond the status quo into the eternal realities of life in the presence of an almighty God (Matt. 5:1- 8:1-3; Luke 4:18-19; John 21:1-19; Acts 1:8; 42-47).

Express your understanding of spiritual authority of the church. Will you share your thoughts on spiritual leadership authority?

There can be no real understanding of the Spiritual Authority of the church, until there is a healthy understanding and respect for the Word of God. The Spiritual Authority of the church cannot exist until there is a wholehearted effort to allow the Word of God to be the final authority in the life of individual believers. In the gospel of John chapter fourteen and verse six (John 14:6), Jesus (the "living" Logos) declares He is the "way" and the "truth" and the "life." Jesus clearly defines how the Word of God is authoritative for the believer and for the church. It is obvious the Word of God establishes the authority of church, because the testimony of His disciples and the multitudes listening to Him preach and teach was simply, "the people were astonished at His teaching, for He taught them as one having authority, and not as the scribes (Matt. 7:28-29; 13:54, KJV). Here lies the key to understanding the false notion that by-laws, policies, procedures, and traditions establish authority. The scribes and Pharisees were in possession of all those things, but it was obvious to the people they lacked the power and authority that comes with an obedient Spirit-filled command of the Word of God (John 7:46). Therefore, spiritual leadership authority is established when a clear stand has been taken to establish the authority of the Word of God through sound Biblical preaching, teaching, and practice.

Share your thoughts on two interrelated models of leadership styles in the church: transformational leadership and servant leadership. Which one has, if any, more value for you as a church pastor? Would you state that you are more likely to embrace one style over the other? Why or why not?

In terms of value and embracing one style over the other, I think characteristics of both styles are mutually beneficial to pastors and should be demonstrated in harmony based on the needs and spiritual maturity of the congregation being served. First, the transformational style of leadership is rooted in consistent Christ-centered Biblical preaching and teaching for "the unity of the faith and the knowledge of the Son of God, to a perfect man, to the measure of the stature of the fullness of Christ." Ephesians chapter four verses eleven through sixteen (Ephesians 4:11-6) explains the full purpose and nature of this leadership style. Whereas, the servant leadership is consistent commitment to service for participation and life within the community of faith. Servant leadership is the premise for Jesus' teaching in the Sermon on the Mount and such passages as Matthew 5:13 where the "saltiness" of the salt is dependent of the "transformational" development of the believer. Just as the brightness of the light in Matthew 5:14-16 is dependent on the "transformational" development of the believer. Matthew chapter nine verses thirty-five through thirty-eight (Matthew 9:35-38), speak to the need for the balance and harmony of both styles of leadership to bring about effective change and uplift for the community that Jesus is concerned about.

What is the pastor's role in church administration?

I will defer and quote Bill Hull here as I have tried to implement the value of the great commission as a leadership and administration model for Indiana Street Missionary Baptist Church for the past ten years and I am starting to harvest some fruit from the seeds that were planted. In Bill Hull's, The Disciple-Making Pastor, he states "Taking the Great Commission seriously means the church leaders themselves are evangelists. They share their faith; they make disciples. As a matter of fact, they were the only considered for leadership because of their years of service as disciple makers. Their main ministry still is disciple making. They have placed it at the heart of the church and do the most important thing in communicating its value; they model it." Every area of the church should be administered from the point of reaching the desired outcome of what we have been commanded to do.

What does this statement mean for you and your congregation: "The pastor serves as change agent?"

For my ministry at Indiana Street Missionary Baptist Church, it means the pastor is the leading disciple-maker and does so by communicating (through preaching/teaching and service) the Biblical principles that lead to spiritual growth and maturity. Most importantly, sharing when God moves you to a new spiritual plane and you not only invite the congregation to move with you, but you challenge and encourage them to move through the continued preaching and teaching of the Word of God with the expectation they will experience their own spiritual "transformation." (Matthew 5:13-16)

Provide expression for this thought, "The cost of leadership."

"A disciple is not above his teacher, nor a servant above his master. It is enough for the disciple to be like his teacher, and the servant like his master. If they have called the master of the house Beelzebul, how much more will they malign those of his household." Matthew 10:24-25 (ESV). If we understand that our service is in the context of the cross of Christ, then we understand it to be the "sacrificial" pouring out of oneself into the life of others for the redemptive knowledge of Jesus Christ and the glory of the Almighty God.

What do you determine to be some competences and essential qualities for effective pastoral leadership?

Essential qualities and competencies for effective pastoral leadership consist of the following:

1. Submission and dependence on the Holy Spirit (John 14:15 – 17:26). In the context of the cross of Christ, I am speaking of humility of faith that gives us access to the genuine grace of God for service to mankind.
2. Knowledge of being free in Christ (Luke 4:18-19; Acts 4:1-31). This liberation allows us to experience the joy of the fulfillment which comes from the presence and power of God.
3. A genuine love and concern for the condition of God's people (Matt. 9:35-38).

Your thoughts on a pastor's personal life and the impact it has on the life and health of a congregation.

"Let this mind be in you which was also in Christ Jesus." Philippians 2:5 KJV
As pastors and spiritual leaders, we have to make a conscious effort to

"die daily to self" and follow Christ; that our lives will be to look like His to the glory of God.

Pastor Derick Easter, New St. Hurricane Missionary Baptist Church, Pine Bluff, AR

Please give your philosophy to biblical visionary leadership as it relates to God's mission and purpose for the church.

Biblical visionary leadership calls us to never lose focus of the greatest example of leadership the world has ever known, Jesus Christ. Practically speaking, as pastor, I must be able to realistically work within the realm of right now, effectively maximizing the resources and personnel I have on hand; but I must also be able, by faith, to see beyond the right now, to a future place and destination that others can't see yet. This means as a biblical visionary leader, as it relates to God's mission and purpose for the church, I must be able to work horizontally, building up and empowering the people I serve, while working vertically, helping to build the kingdom of God at the same time.

Express your understanding of spiritual authority for the church. Will you share your thoughts on spiritual leadership authority?

I believe that all believers possess spiritual authority. In Ephesians, Paul prayed that believers would grasp the depth and breadth of their authority in Jesus Christ.

When it comes to spiritual leadership authority, the Bible teaches that legitimate leaders have authority and that the authority comes from God and is given to His leaders for the good of the church. There are numerous scriptures that teach that leaders should be respected and obeyed when operating within their legitimate sphere of authority. I don't think this means that there is never disagreement. Disagreement can be healthy as long as it is expressed in a way that safeguards the unity of the church and is done in a respectful and not angry manner. This is different than rebellion. Rebellion against spiritual leadership authority that causes division and schism is sinful.

Share your thoughts on two interrelated models of leadership styles in the church: transformational leadership and servant leadership. Which one has, if any, more value for you as a church pastor? Would you state that you are more likely to embrace one style over the other? Why or why not?

I realize that these are two separate but related leadership styles, but I honestly believe that I operate almost equally in both. As Pastor I believe my primary style is servant leadership. A servant leader places the good of the followers over his self-interest in working to help others. Transformational leaders work to raise the level of motivation and morality on the team to innovate and create change.

I want to begin as a servant leader who places the good of others above myself as I serve those in our church and outside of our church but I also want to be a transformational leader that constantly challenges people that I lead to think beyond where we already are and motivate them to what we can and should be.

What is the pastor's role in church administration?

Of course, the pastor's primary role is preaching, teaching and pastoral care. While the pastor also serves as the chief administrator of the church how that administration is carried out differs from church to church. I think it should be done in a way to free the pastor to do his primary roles to the best of his ability; that could mean hiring an executive pastor, bringing in additional lay volunteers, hiring a full time/part time administrative assistant, and leaning on the trustees in the care of the property. Again, I believe the pastor is the chief administration and should be kept in the loop; but it is a regrettable oversight if the congregation wants that to be his primary role and not that of preaching and teaching.

What does this statement mean for you and your congregation: "The pastor serves as change agent?"

I really do believe the best leaders are accustomed to leading change. There are some leaders that are gifted change agents that have the rare ability to lead through change. I believe that the pastor must serve as a change agent as we are trying to affect change in people and communities.

Provide expression for this thought, "The cost of leadership."

This is a reminder that leadership comes with a price. The cost is financial, emotional, physical, spiritual and personal.

What do you determine to be some competences & essential qualities for effective pastoral leadership?

I think the Bible adequately covers the qualifications for those who lead a congregation of people as senior pastor. I think if one considers Titus chapter 1, 1 Tim chapter 3:

- ➤ A pastor must be devoted to his wife; one-woman man (Titus 1:6; 1 Tim 3:2, ESV).
- ➤ A pastor's children must be in submission, though not perfect (Titus 1:6; 1 Tim 3:4-5, ESV).
- ➤ A pastor is a faithful steward (Titus 1:7, ESV).
- ➤ A pastor must be humble — not arrogant (Titus 1:7, ESV)
- ➤ A pastor must be gentle — not quick-tempered (Titus 1:7; 1 Tim 3:3).
- ➤ A pastor must be sober — not a drunkard (Titus 1:7; 1 Tim 3:3, ESV).
- ➤ A pastor must be peaceful — not violent (Titus 1:7; 1 Tim 3:3, ESV).
- ➤ A pastor must have financial integrity — not greedy for gain (Titus 1:7; 1 Tim 3:3; 1 Peter 5:3, ESV).
- ➤ A pastor must be hospitable (Titus 1:8; 1 Tim 3:2, ESV).
- ➤ A pastor must be a lover of good (Titus 1:8, ESV).
- ➤ A pastor must be self-controlled (Titus 1:8; 1 Tim 3:2, ESV).
- ➤ A pastor must be upright (Titus 1:8, ESV).
- ➤ A pastor must be holy (Titus 1:8, ESV).
- ➤ A pastor must be able to teach (Titus 1:9; 1 Tim 3:2, ESV).
- ➤ A pastor must be spiritually mature (1 Tim 3:6, ESV).
- ➤ A pastor must be respectable (1 Tim 3:7, ESV).
- ➤ A pastor must be an example to the flock (1 Peter 5:3, ESV).

Your thoughts on a pastor's personal life and the impact it has on the life and health of a congregation.

If a pastor isn't careful the success of his ministry could also mean the failure of his family. Personally, I think I have a hard time finding a good balance between church and family. Honestly speaking, there are times when I am home that I am not home. I am praying and intentionally seeking balance between leading our congregation and having a healthy personal life. The reality is that sometimes those struggling with anxiety and depression are those leading the church. Statistics say that one in five adults experience mental illness each year.

We are seeing a disturbing trend of pastor's committing suicide because of the reality of mental illness. I think that Pastor's must give attention to a healthy personal life and congregations must be active in suggesting or demanding that pastor's take time they need to refresh, as well as take time to work on their marriages so that they can return and lead the congregation well. The Pastor's personal life certainly has an impact, positively or negatively, on the life and health of the congregation.

Pastor Amelio P. Howard, Grace Temple Missionary Baptist Church, Pine Bluff, AR

Please give your philosophy to biblical visionary leadership as it relates to God's mission and purpose for the church.

I believe biblical visionary leadership is looking both ways; looking toward heaven, awaiting revelation, and looking within self, waiting on God for inspiration, information and direction. I believe the leader should allow God, through the Holy Spirit, to look through his/her spiritual eyes, to enable him/her to envision, within his/her spirit, God's mission and purpose for the church.

Express your understanding of spiritual authority for the church. Will you share your thoughts on spiritual leadership authority?

The Spirit of the living God should be recognized, honored, obeyed and followed. "The Spirit" is an intelligent being who gives direction and provides guidance to the Pastor for the purpose of leading the membership according to the Word of God.

Share your thoughts on two interrelated models of leadership styles in the church: transformational leadership and servant leadership. Which one has, if any, more value for you as a church pastor? Would you state that you are more likely to embrace one style over the other? Why or why not?

Transformational leadership is where the pastor creates teams to help identify need for change, how to implement the change and evaluate the change. In my opinion, transformational leadership is leadership that is horizontal in style or flat leadership – across on the same level. Transformational leadership is the team network concept; information is being shared from team to team. For example: Pastor – deacon ministry – young adults – singles – couples – new members.

Servant leadership is a "coach" style leadership. Pastor, as a servant leader, shares power and gets in the trenches with members or gets on the front-line hand in hand with the members. The servant leader is open to listening and sharing information. I am a servant leader. I encourage, support and embrace suggestions and ideas. I believe "the coach," the pastor should lead by example. I have the mentality of "do as I do and not as I say."

On the flipside, in today's changing world, the Pastor should be flexible enough to adapt to both leadership styles at any given moment. In the Black

MARGARETTE W. WILLIAMS, ED.D., PH.D.

Baptist church, the dynamics could change generationally because each generation brings about different challenges. The Pastor should be open, flexible and willing to change, as long as the gospel is not compromised.

What is the pastor's role in church administration?

The pastor's role in church administration is important because the pastor is an agent of the church, the face of the Church, the leader of the church and ex-officio. The pastor's role in church administration should be spirit-led to lead the congregation as a "coach"; through motivation and leading by example.

What does this statement mean for you and your congregation: "The pastor serves as change agent?"

The pastor must be flexible in an ever-changing world. The pastor must be opened to listening, reasoning and adjusting, without compromising the gospel. The pastor must be able to reach all members of all age groups and generations through preaching, teaching, and singing while holding fast to the core principles of the church. The pastor must be able to lead all members to respect each generation's point-of-view of carrying out the mission of the church. The seasoned saints must be willing to listen to and respect the younger generation; by the same token, the younger generation must be willing to listen and respect the seasoned generation as they come to the understanding, salvation is for all, regardless of age or generation. The pastor must be willing and able to bridge the gap between both generations while preserving the value and core mission of the church with respect to everyone.

Provide expression for this thought, "The cost of leadership."

The cost of leadership means self-denial. It is compromising without compromising the gospel. The cost of leadership means a spotlight is being placed in the leader's life and/or a bull's eye is being placed on the leader's back which means the leader must be willing to be transparent; having a good name within and without the church.

What do you determine to be some competences & essential qualities for effective pastoral leadership?

Lifestyle, commitment, being an example, being God-lead, being faithful, and meeting parishioners where they are should be considered as competences and essential qualities for effective pastoral leadership.

Your thoughts on a pastor's personal life and the impact it has on the life and health of a congregation.

In life, people remember what the pastor does rather than what the pastor says. Christians (congregations) are willing to follow a pastor who is living what he preaches. There is truth to the old cliché "action speaks louder than words." Christians (congregations) are proud of their pastors whose lives are above reproach.

Pastor Ronald Laurent, First Missionary Baptist Church, Holly Grove, AR

1. Please give your philosophy to Biblical visionary leadership as it relates to God's mission and purpose for the church.

My philosophy of biblical visionary leadership is servant leadership where we are seeing the future clearly by doing the work of discipleship for our Lord, Jesus Christ. The mission and purpose of the church is to make disciples for Christ. Therefore, the leader of the local congregation must become a spiritual equipper so the body can do the work of ministry which leads to building up the body of Christ.

Express your understanding of spiritual authority for the church.

The spiritual authority for the church is God. The church belongs to Him. Jesus paid the cost for our salvation with His death on Calvary.

Will you share your thoughts on spiritual leadership authority?

As a pastor, I am a steward whose spiritual leadership comes from God. The authority for Spiritual Leadership is based on scripture. Paul tells the elders in Ephesus, "Take heed therefore unto yourselves, and to all the flock, over the which the Holy Ghost hath made you overseers, to feed the church of Good, which he hath purchased with His own blood" (Acts 20:28, KJV). Therefore, pastors must use influence that is biblically based.

Share your thoughts on two interrelated models of leadership styles in the church: transformational leadership and servant leadership. Which one has, if any, more value for you as a church pastor? Would you state that you are more likely to embrace one style over the other? Why or why not?

I must first define each of these leadership models. Both definitions come from Wikipedia. Servant-leadership_is a leadership philosophy in which the main goal of the leader is to serve. Transformational leadership is a theory of leadership where a leader works with teams to identify needed change, creating a vision to guide the change through inspiration. At this point in my pastorate, transformational leadership is more valuable to me. I am in the midst of transitioning to use transformational leadership, because of a need to bring about change in our congregation.

What is the pastor's role in church administration?

The role of the pastor in church administration is leadership. In the Hebrew, the word for pastor in the Bible means to tend to a flock. Therefore, the pastor must demonstrate love for the congregation so that the members of the congregation will follow. Leadership at its basic level is simply influence.

What does this statement mean for you and your congregation: "The pastor serves as change agent?"

If change is to take place, the pastor must influence the congregation to change. The pastor must lead the way toward change.

Provide expression for this thought, "The cost of leadership."

The cost of leadership is a sacrificial cost. As a pastor, we are required to follow the example of Christ. The Lord has committed the oversight (leadership) of the church to pastors. Therefore, we must yield to the will of God and deny our personal desires. Jesus said in Matthew 16:24 (KJV), "... If any man will come after me, let him deny himself, and take up his cross, and follow me."

What do you determine to be some competences & essential qualities for effective pastoral leadership?

The essential qualities are given to us in 1st Timothy 3:1-7 and Titus 1:5-9. Some competences that enhance the effectiveness of pastoral leaderships are: effective communication skills (oral and written), interpersonal skills-the ability to appropriately interact with the congregation; a fervent prayer life; and a commitment to the study of the Word of God.

Your thoughts on a pastor's personal life and the impact it has on the life and health of a congregation.

A pastor's personal life must be one that must align with 1st Timothy 3:1-7 and Titus 1:5-9. Because the pastor is a visible example for the congregation, his personal life must be above reproach. This will eliminate distractions by the congregation, so the mission and ministry of the church can go forth.

Rev. Gardiner L. Sanders, Mercy Seat Missionary Baptist Church, Little Rock, AR

Please give your philosophy to biblical visionary leadership as it relates to God's mission and purpose for the church.

When we talk about vision for the church, we may actually be looking for the mind of a leader to give us just that. We ask ourselves "how can we have vision." We build buildings to leave a great legacy, but what is vision? How will man have vision? The mandate of Christ is the vision for the local church and the church at large. Scripture gives structure for vision for the local assembly. Vision is not given to the intellectual, as a means to espouse greatness or grandeur, but vision is the coalition of what the Spirit of God desires to happen between the local assembly, and the leader placed in charge to bridge these two together. Vision is what pulls these two together. Vision is what God says in His Word, how His leader presents it before His people and how the people of God trust and believe to receive and obey what has been visualized and taught.

Express your understanding of spiritual authority for the church.

Spiritual authority is best termed as biblical authority. It has to do with what authority from the Bible is given to the church. The Bible gives spiritual authority to both pastors and there are spiritual mandates given to members. In Matthew 28:18, (KJV), it is written that "all power is given in heaven and in earth." We often start at verse 19 which states "to go," but in doing so, we take the full message away from its intended context. The interpretation of the text is to include all of it, literally. We cannot leave the power of the Holy Spirit behind. The task is that spiritual authority is over everything and everyone in the church. The church's influence in society is most valuable. When I talk about spiritual authority over all things, I am relating even to governance. Not to interfere or impede but to still get the job that the church must do, done. The church has spiritual authority to govern itself in spiritual matters. Matthew 5 reminds us that "ye are salt and light (Matthew 5:13-14, NIV)." As relating to spiritual leadership authority, the Lord designated, dispensationally, how he wanted leadership to perform. Even before the church age, in the Old Testament, we see God's leadership dispensationally change as he wanted it to change. The local church deals with government, church polity, pastors, deacons, and other lay leaders. That's the piece that is hurting us so much; power struggle over positions. These struggles bring about abuse in leadership

Share your thoughts on two interrelated models of leadership styles in the church: transformational leadership and servant leadership. Which one has, if any, more value for you as a church pastor? Would you state that you are more likely to embrace one style over the other? Why or why not?

They are demonstratively different but equally needed in the operation and furtherance of the kingdom for the church. Personally, I do not think picking one as greater or embracing one over the other serves to produce leadership as we need for the congregation. I think the problem is when you separate them, you risk losing the order you need with developing true servants. Point here is that we need servants who have been transformed! People who have not been transformed will not serve. They will perform or substitute, but they will not serve. A person who is not transformed is a substitute worker, but still must become a true servant. Only a transformed Christian will become a servant.

What is the pastor's role in church administration?

The pastor's role in church administration is to facilitate its existence. Administration has the idea of movement, mobility, of reaching and connecting one thing or people with each other. Administration brings continuity with reaching a set goal or the agreed upon mission of the organization. In this case, the mission and goals of the church require adequate administration to succeed with bringing them to pass. The pastor has been given a biblical assignment to take oversight. That model comes from the family model as described in scripture. Pastors make sure administration happens. We recall in Acts 6:3 (KJV) that the Apostles suggested to the church to appoint "men of honest report, who were full of the Holy Ghost and wisdom," to handle the business of the church. This was to ensure that the Apostles would give themselves "continually to prayer, and to the ministry of the word."

What does this statement mean for you and your congregation: "The pastor serves as change agent?"

I should be the one who is the greatest promoter of change as it relates to the local church. Change that happens inside the church should end up being change that also affects society and the surrounding community at large. It is necessary that effective change go beyond the walls of the local assembly. For example, having college students in worship, or inviting community school sports teams are examples of providing a voice outward to the community, which is part of our end goal, reaching the masses. Our call is to serve this present age. It is not a self-serving call; if we have selfish motives, we become serf-serving and are not fulfilling our call to this present age.

Provide expression for this thought, "The cost of leadership."

The cost of leadership is obedience. You are not really a leader if you are not a follower. The life of Dr. Martin Luther King is a great example. Dr. King was a leader but his greatest triumph as well as his greatest tragedy was that he led people by using scripture. His approach to injustice was not one of violence but rather, he used an approach that led him to great harm. He was beaten, jailed, and his life came to an early demise. Obedience is our greatest need in leadership. To stand as a leader, one has to stand alone. People do not see nor do they always appreciate the vision. Some people are totally against the vision. Sometimes these can be people within your immediate circle who will break down on you.

What do you determine to be some competences & essential qualities for effective pastoral leadership?

Availability is vital to the office of a pastor. The work takes a lot of time; knowing the ability and skills of the people to help serve in ministry is equally important. People often want to be leaders; they feel that leaders are born with the capacity to lead well. Another factor is the ability to accept abuse. Abuse in leadership is not all that uncommon. Leadership comes from the life of Jesus! He knew His abilities and His challenges. He was able to accept abuse. Observe the struggle and the humanity of Christ during a time in the garden of Gethsemane. Leaders cannot maintain a soft skin; they cannot wear their feelings on their sleeve.

Your thoughts on a pastor's personal life and the impact it has on the life and health of a congregation.

A pastor's personal life is biblical but not boring. Self-care must come first. Pastors should not live the life where laughter has been left out. Some pastors never unplug. Pastors are always "preachers." They are preachers in the community, the church and the family; but it should not only about those things in ministry. Life needs to mirror the context, such as was portrayed by the Master. Do not become overzealous. The pastor's personal life should be an example, but not the example.

Pastor Roderick Smith, Centennial Missionary Baptist Church, Kensett, AR

Please give your philosophy to biblical visionary leadership as it relates to God's mission and purpose for the church.

Our vision should come straight from God and line up with scripture. It's hard to find your point without it lining up with the scriptures. This is the first and most important factor in teaching and leading. Believers must know that it is not about you, but that your leadership and teaching is for the betterment of the overall body of believers. As a body of believers, we come together in vision to bring changes in the church and the community. We do not stand alone. Our foundation is in God's Word and Its power to change people for good. Pastors preach to prove scripture without changing the context.

Express your understanding of Spiritual Authority for the church.

God has a divine design for His church. Spiritual authority for the church comes from pastoral leadership and is passed down to the congregation. God gives the vision to the leader and the leader delivers God's message to the people. From Amos 3:7 (KJV), "God does nothing in the earth without first revealing His secrets to His servants, the prophets".

Share your thoughts on two interrelated models of leadership styles in the church: transformational leadership and servant leadership. Which one has, if any, more value for you as a church pastor? Would you state that you are more likely to embrace one style over the other? Why or why not?

Transformational Leadership is sharing your leadership skills with others in order to transform others in the service of the church. Transformational leadership has more value for my congregation. For example, if something happens to the pastor, ministry continues to go on. I emphasize servant leaders because of its value to set the example of the pastor before the church.

What is the pastor's role in church administration?

I believe the Pastor's role in church administration is to give oversight to the overall function of operations for the entire body. Personally, I would rather not be a micro manager. At the same time, it is good practice to hold others' (for lack of a better phrase) "feet to the fire" to make sure they follow through for the benefit of the church.

What does this statement mean for you and your congregation: "The pastor serves as change agent?"

I believe changes in church structure should come through the Pastor. While I believe vision comes from the Pastor, I also believe good ideas for change can come from others as they seek leadership from the pastor.

Provide expression for this thought, "The cost of leadership."

Leadership comes with a high cost. It is about what is called "the accountability factor." Whether I like it or not, I am accountable for everything that happens in the church; it comes back on me. If one is not willing to pay the cost, that individual should not be in pastoral leadership.

What do you determine to be some competences & essential qualities for effective pastoral leadership?

Effective qualities for pastoral leaders include the opportunity to seek and develop value in kingdom living in others. To be able to bring forth spiritual qualities for leading others to a new walk with Christ is one of the many goals of effective pastoral teaching and preaching. It is important to make plain to the people of God, His vision and hope for His church.

Your thoughts on a Pastor's Personal Life and the impact it has on the life and health of a congregation.

To have a personal life away from the church that people will respect is an essential part of pastoral care. A pastor's example of a good personal life allows members to pursue a good personal life from the example the leader has previously set. I believe a pastor's personal life must be as blemish free as possible. The pastor lives from the creed of the Apostle Paul that says to members, "imitate me as I imitate Christ." This is a Christ like life.

Again, thank you to each pastor for your major and unselfish gift of kindness, diligence, and your hard work to the successful completion of Chapter Five. May your reward of selfless servant sacrifice be great on earth as it is in heaven!

Misuse and Abuses in Leadership

An understated power of negative influence has been found to be operating in the church. Described as spiritual abuse and in some instances misuse, this force appears in many forms and shows up in the most unlikely of places. *Spiritual leadership* abuse occurs when clever leaders, operating from their role as agents of spiritual authority, attempt to rule with behaviors that manipulate, control, shame, or condemn persons within the congregation. These acts of abuse lead to exploitation in leadership and the mismanagement of power in church conduct and worship. When forms of abuse occur, punishments have been found in members' loss of privileges, often by shunning, or even in expulsion when a submission to conform is not met.

Another area called misuse has been traced to a variety of actions in the form of spiritual manipulation.[40] Spiritual manipulation occurs when people negotiate, control, or influence for their own advantage. Spiritual manipulation results from actions of a pastor, a teacher or even a member in the congregation to use false teachings from scripture in ways to control how members interpret or think about what the Bible is saying. Misplaced loyalties and the overemphasis on individualized performance for personal enrichment or gratuities are also examples of spiritual manipulation within the church.

There are also times when cases of misuse have been a part of the congregational culture. Misuse of privileges has been observed when devious church members, persons who have been provided a certain amount of authority, attempt to use their leverage to control other members in their groups or on their teams. These individuals may even try to control the pastor in order to win advantages in ministry or leadership. These methods are used to ensure other members' obedience to personal desires or ambitious gain in the church.

Pastor Guns identified what he termed as one of the "most critical and pressing leadership problems in traditional church congregations." He labeled the problem as "spiritual tyranny or rebellion."[41] Issues of this nature occur when leaders use their spiritual positions to control and dominate others. Outbreaks of rebellion can appear in the pulpit; however, pastors will also experience unruly, difficult church members from within the pews.

The church of believers has always dealt with subtle and oftentimes not so obvious ways to reject the spiritual leadership of Godly pastors in the administration of their duties for the good of the congregation. Many pastors and their families have suffered needlessly from persons within the church who have intentionally set to disrupt the order and spirit of the congregation. This conduct is out of order and is contrary to the commands of God for the spiritual edification in the church.

Actions of misconduct can lead to long term negative consequences for the people of God if they are not controlled from the position of the pulpit or from righteous insight and the prayers of members in the congregation. Church leaders can benefit from principles and strategies for pastors and members to recognize and overcome the spirits of rebellion, abuse, and misuse at all levels in the church.

None of these forces of negative influence align with God's plan for promoting spiritual maturity or discipleship. In fact, they hinder the power of the Spirit of Christ from fully operating within the congregation.

Leadership Pitfalls

Scripture, when paired with education, training, and experiences, provides pastors and church leaders with wisdom and knowledge to carry out their God ordained callings for the church. Because God has placed a great value on the worth, as well as the duties of pastors; they must certainly care for their flock as they shepherd the church of God (Acts 20:28, KJV). There is a higher standard to personal accountability assigned to church leaders (Hebrews 13:17) who have been called to lead, guide, and watch over the souls of many. While all members are called to righteous living, greater responsibility is weighted to those leading and influencing others in building the kingdom.

In 1 Peter 5:1-4 (KJV), elders (pastors, rulers and bishops), those persons belonging to the office of individuals appointed to feed and oversee the flock of Christ, were reminded of the gravity of their office and the weight of accountability given to their charge to instruct and care for persons within the congregations. Peter summed his own personal journey as one who was "a witness of the sufferings of Christ," but yet at the time of his writings he noted that he also "suffered with Him."

A powerful point to keep in mind is that persons who serve as clergy; shepherds of the earthly flock, men and women who suffer with Christ for the sake of the kingdom, will one day be redeemed to God by the Great Shepherd. St. Peter wanted these leaders, as well as pastors of the gospel today, to know and to receive respect in the knowledge that they were called for such a great work. They had been given a title of favor to lead and to render special service to His people. What an honor to have been charged by the authority of the Chief Shepherd, the Chief Cornerstone, the Great Prince of Pastors, to exercise their "office of elder" in His name. In glory, pastors and rulers and bishops will receive a crown of righteousness that will never fade away.

What a blessing! However, counter to the greatness of the office of elder, is the ever-present concern with pitfalls and dangers generally associated with a call to leadership. There are skills and a mindset many leaders, especially young pastors, may not have acquired in an awareness to recognize problems that could exist along the way. There are troubles to destroy or bring to ruin much of the good God has provided for them. Pitfalls in leadership are always present.

A pitfall can be identified as a hidden or not easily recognizable danger or difficulty. These hard to recognize sources of peril or trouble are usually unsuspecting to many novice leaders who lack the necessary wisdom or foresight to confront the trouble and move away. There are likewise, other contributing factors or causes that can lead to negative consequences for a Christian leader. Pitfalls also include the need for pride, ambition, or fame. These fault lines in character can be major contributors to mistakes and poor decision making by both unsuspecting new or otherwise unyielding older or even more seasoned leaders.

Dangers (Pitfalls) for Church Pastors, Elders and Leaders

The following is a list of dangers I perceive church leaders may face at some point in the work of their leadership. Some of these are somewhat more difficult to manage than others. The wisdom of scripture, wise counsel from elders in the church, and the individual's personal commitment to truth will lessen the occurrence of these errors and their negative impact to ministry from the lives of godly leaders.

➤ Pitfalls in not fully understanding the gravity of the Calling.
➤ Pitfalls with an inability to grasp vision for the church.
➤ Pitfalls in rightly communicating the gospel message.
➤ Pitfalls in not acquiring necessary leadership skills and strategies for the work.
➤ Pitfalls of desiring personal gain over stewardship and sacrifice.
➤ Pitfalls with pride and ambition.

➢ Pitfalls with neglecting to seek God's favor for the hope of the church.
➢ Pitfalls with desiring personal acceptance from man.
➢ Pitfalls in the willingness to condemn many for the flaws of a few.
➢ Pitfalls in not understanding the dynamics surrounding difficult members.
➢ Pitfalls in dealing (or not dealing) with messy issues in the church.
➢ Pitfalls with neglecting to embrace counsel from seasoned leaders who serve well.
➢ Pitfalls with desiring too much too soon.
➢ Pitfalls in understanding ministry needs to train and mentor new leaders for service.
➢ Pitfalls with planning for ongoing organization and structural dynamics.
➢ Pitfalls with limited knowledge of the role of Christian education in the church.
➢ Pitfalls with limited skills in church administration and management.
➢ Pitfalls in one's personal life.

❖

CHAPTER SIX

Leadership Planning for Ministry

Effective Spiritual Leadership

After having received God's promises of blessings and redemption, Abraham, the first Hebrew patriarch, submitted to God's message of obedience for his family and himself. God's declaration to Abraham that he would become the "Father of many nations (Genesis 17:4, KJV)" is realized today in salvation and faith through Jesus Christ. All who believe and trust regardless of ancestry or creed, are partakers of the privileges gained from the household of Abraham. Whether of Jewish lineage of Hebrew, Greek, or of Gentile origin, belief emanating from these early acts of faith and obedience allows us to share in the inheritance through Christ our Lord. Abraham is indeed a father to the faithful. He so believed to the point that *"God counted his faith as righteousness* (Romans 4:3, KJV)." Abraham and all who follow in his faithfulness are sons and daughters of righteousness and friends of God.

What an absolute encouragement to the church when leaders can be counted on to maintain a continued devotion to the mission of salvation, God's saving faith for discipleship in kingdom service. Pastors and leaders who maintain a focus toward Calvary with their gaze on Christ, acquire sharp skills to prepare their people in a continuous search for the one true mission God has for the church.

Throughout the Bible, examples of leaders are provided to record their works, their actions, and give insight into their character. The multiplicity of demands, the increasing numbers of souls to care for and the numerous decisions to guide, instruct and command, all require a continuous thread of new and experienced persons to step up and lead.

Oswald Sanders, in his book, Spiritual Leadership [42] wrote about how God choose and equipped individuals to lead. Obligations common to planning quality leadership include recruiting persons who possess motivation to commit to full discipleship, to take on the responsibility to mentor others for service, and individuals who are willing to be used to the limit. Although leaders may themselves have short comings, naturally because they are human, key points to remember is that regardless of their limitations, spiritual leaders serve God with wholeheartedly good intent.

Mike Ayers wrote of five distinctive characteristics Christian leaders should possess. From his perspective, leaders are individuals uniquely suited to advance the spiritual kingdom in the church. In his book, *Power to Lead: Five Essentials for the Practice of Biblical Leaders,* [43] he communicated that at the center of all great efforts in leading is one's ability to lead from the heart.

Leading from the love of Jesus positions leaders to discover the basic truth for why they lead to perfect all they have been assigned to accomplish. Their leadership style is a walk of faith to hold on to the teachings of the One who saves and delivers followers. Leaders, who follow a scriptural way to summon others for service, are influencers of hope for all who are reconciled into God's gift of redemption.

Biblical Mandate to Plan for Leadership in Ministry[44]

Passages of scripture identify texts for developing leaders, equipping them for service and for teaching models of excellence in leadership style. Answers to develop skills in leadership are found in the Word of God. Read His Word to research primary sources about what leadership means to the church. Jesus's example and His style in leadership are uniquely transparent for leaders to mentor and to follow His many models for leading.

Whether a leader's experiences are seasoned by years of decision-making opportunities or they exist from the works of newer novice leaders, seeking answers to a multiplicity of ecumenical concerns is always in order. The biblical authority of God's Word is faithful.

Listed here are a few Bible verses to help leaders understand what God says to leaders today:

Luke 6:31 (NIV) Do to others as you would like them to do to you.

Philippians 2:3 (NLT) Don't be selfish; don't try to impress others. Be humble, thinking of others as better than yourselves.

Proverbs 4:23 (NLT) Guard your heart above all else, for it determines the course of your life.

Exodus 18:21 (NIV) But select capable men from all the people—men who fear God, trustworthy men who hate dishonest gain —and appoint them as officials over thousands, hundreds, fifties and tens.

Psalm 78:72 (ESV) With upright heart he shepherded them and guided them with his skillful hand.

Matthew 20:26 (NLT) But among you it will be different. Whoever wants to be a leader among you must be your servant."

Philippians 2:4 (NLT) Do not look out only for your own interests, but take on an interest in others, too.

Matthew 5:37 (NIV) All you need to say is simply "Yes" or "No"; anything beyond this comes from the evil one.

Effective Leadership is Character Driven

Thirty-six years in community and church leadership ministry has afforded me personal insight into qualities essential to effective leadership. A list of leadership skills consistent with building strength and endurance in character is included at the end of this section. When leaders pursue completion of assignments to task, aspects of character in personality are noticed from the leaders's personal messaging and style. Factors that determine how a leader is perceived, respected, admired, or even shunned are often related to the impact the leader's personality has on the spirit of the organization.

Qualities of effective leaders include the positivity of their self esteem and their ability to look out for the interests of the group. Effective leaders find time to spend moments sharing and communicating with those they desire to influence. These leaders are focus driven, but recognize the importance of bringing the team along with them to enhance project vision and design. While these particulars do not detail the full matter to planning for leaders, they are valuable to setting critical groundwork for operating in basic leadership proficiencies in preparation for excellence in ministry development.

Leadership takes courage, discipline and determination. From the writings of each pastor noted in Chapter Five, great leadership comes with significant cost. Leaders are often overcome with the weight of insurmountable details to task, one after the other. Christian leaders who submit to truth are aware that integrity is the foundational brick to building character required for sustained quality service.

Numerous examples in scripture detail how God spoke to encourage men and women who were chosen to lead. Effective leaders allow character, reliability, honor, respectability, and truth to stand out as guiding forces of their inspiration.

Consider the following list of ten characteristics of high-quality leadership:

> A leader submits to the will and authority of God.
> A leader serves for the good of others.
> A leader leads by example.
> A leader takes the greater risks.
> A leader sees the big picture; carefully considering options beyond the obvious.
> A leader plans for the unexpected.
> A leader has integrity, standards and character of worth.
> A leader willingly shares knowledge with likeminded followers.
> A leader does not fear the gifts, talents and abilities of others.
> A leader recognizes that the whole is far greater than the sum of individual parts.
> A leader may give out but strives to not give up. A leader considers God's guidance to know when a particular service has been completed.

Excellence in character for leadership is nothing short of transforming lives through obedience and submission to God's commands to love and to seek peace with those served in the command of duty. Leaders must be aware of the influence of their speech since words have power to heal or to harm. The desire to seek peace in harmony with others establishes relationships in the continuous coordination of responsibilities leading to securing joy and hope; even in the difficult places and during the most challenging of times.

Leaders are Made or Born?

I simply refuse to take an unwarranted amount of space to write on the heading: Are Leaders Made or Born? There is so much discussion back and forth in the research, and basically all of it says or ends with the same conclusion: Leaders are born. Leaders are made. "Which came first, the chicken or the egg?"

Spending the greater part of the past forty-five years of my life in graduate schools to earn professional credentialing from public speaking communication, to therapeutic speech language pathology, to education administration, higher education administration, and finally to global ministry leadership, I dare not utter that I only believe that leaders are born! Great goals are usually obtained through meticulous work, hard study, and life experiences. The diligent life possesses a massive amount of tenacity in the pursuit of creativity and talent.

Many leaders are usually thought of as lifelong learners. As students to obtain all that life could offer, they often *graduate to* some other form of schooling or training for new learning to improve their skills. Scripture teaches that Iron sharpens Iron (Proverbs 27:17, KJV). The principle is that learning with others supports the growth, wisdom and skills acquired through collaboration with others. Christ took it upon himself to teach, mold and shape the lives of His twelve disciples along with the countless others who followed Him.

For three years, Jesus led by teaching, training, modeling, and in some instances, rebuking. In time, each disciple became like Him in his own way. They were transformed to His likeness as a result of being direct recipients of His message and His delivery.

A commentary illustrating the significance of the disciples' following of Christ is presented by author and blogger Scott Williams, a key leader and Campus Pastor.[45] As a passionate writer and developer of organizational growth and diversity, Williams blogged about the status of leadership skills the disciples possessed when Jesus first met them. Williams's summation that "I think, *Leaders are born to be made*" was his uncomplicated view to settle the issue of the manifestation of their transformation from his perspective of thought.

The disciples grew in some amazing skills for endurance and commitment to all that Jesus taught. They walked into the academy of His tutelage possessing the trade skills from their individual professions. For three years they spent time learning the life of discipleship for kingdom building as a result of their call into His service. Following their matriculation in school with Christ, they had obtained wisdom, knowledge, and discernment from experiences while serving with the Lord.

I think simply, leaders are born to become all that their skills, abilities, education, appropriate training, and leading from the Holy Spirit will enable the call on their lives to produce.

Effective leadership requires training and continuous enablement in new principles and strategies of knowledge to pair with sound judgment in management. Equipping leaders for service is a process of development from varied and diverse models of leaders' tools necessary for the right training. Training in communication, self awareness, organizational management, and personal enrichment are valuable byproducts in skill building for advanced operational leadership.

The Excellent Leader

Pastors and their leadership teams are usually the targets of very watchful eyes. As with all organizations, the church is going to receive its fair share of opportunities to "discuss the leader." Those who serve with the pastor in leadership roles are also subject to careful scrutiny from others within the congregation. The "you are in the heat of the kitchen" paradigm is always operational, even in the church. Leaders are reminded that their mission to the call is to influence others to live obediently in Christ. It could be that in many instances, leaders, and most importantly, the pastor, are the first form of Christ a congregation will see.

So, what makes a good leader? Among many other qualities previously mentioned, excellence in leadership will also mean to lead by example. Supported by scripture, a biblical review of what it means to become an example of leadership is provided in this section.

To be an example for others, leaders must first know that they indeed are followers of Christ. The only legitimate expectations Christian leaders can place on people to follow them is when they are following the life of Jesus; from His teachings to His examples. Excellent sources to obtain how to acquire a mindset to become like Jesus are found from the writings of the apostles of the New Testament. Listed below are scriptural references to study in order to glean instances of exceptional leadership styles as exemplified by our Lord Christ.

Much is owed to an understanding of how mentoring and serving as an example of Christ is expressed through the writings of the Apostles Paul, Peter and John, as they each share their message of Christ to the church. These men of authority and power stand as giants of super models of godly men who served with hearts full for Christ. Several scriptures are listed for this writing:

> John 13:15 (NIV) - *Jesus:* "I have set you an example that you should do as I have done for you."

> 1 Corinthians 11:1 (NIV) - *Apostle Paul:* "Follow my example, as I follow the example of Christ."

The next list of scriptures specifically reference *Christ* as our example to follow in leadership:

> John 13:15; Phil. 2:5-8 (NIV) - In humility, indicates how to treat people with the heart of a servant in perseverance.

> 1 Peter 2:21; Heb. 12:1-4 (NIV).

The next scriptures are listed to indicate how to endure in suffering or adverse circumstances without losing joy:

> 1 Timothy 4:12; 2 Thess. 3:7; Titus 2:7-8 (NIV).[46]

Leaders, who secure a lifestyle of virtue, possess desirable qualities in goodness, righteousness, and honesty. Attitudes of superior quality will influence others to seek and to serve with likeminded worth. The prayer "Help Lord" is a necessary plea for persons aspiring to become a church leader and for those who are presently serving in the role of leadership at their church or place of worship. Seeking divine wisdom from Christ encompasses much that is noble and is the end to all that is virtuous and uprightly inspired by God for the greater good on behalf of others.

The Leader Sets the Example

John Maxwell wrote that the ultimate test of leadership is in the creation of positive change.[47] A familiar quote, cited from the Greek philosopher, Heraclitus, is that "there is only one constant in life, and that constant is change." For this late sixth century Greek philosopher,[48] failure to experience wisdom from life's occurrences often leads to difficulties in making decisions to move forward. This indecisiveness leads to unnecessary mishaps for the second step, and for movements beyond. Eventually, everything is going to change. Nothing remains the same.

Instead of just trusting one's own initial thoughts when facing difficult situations, the first actions of sound leadership ought to be to seek the counsel of the Lord. Follow Proverbs 3:5, (KJV), to "trust in the Lord with all thine heart and to lean not unto thine own understanding, but in all thine ways, acknowledge Him and He will direct our paths." Mindful leaders intentionally create environments of good will that please God for producing admirable and favorable outcomes.

This kind of leading sets the example to bring glory that is pleasing to God. Again, this is leading from a heart for God. Although he was not perfect in all of his actions and certainly, some of his decisions were questionable, David, the young King, and also in his older years, lived to please the Lord. He wholeheartedly loved and trusted his God. His heart of adoration to God was the foundation for his best actions. God says of David, "I have found David, son of Jesse, a man after my own heart; he will do everything I want him to do" (Acts 13:22, NIV). These actions require the wisdom written about in (James 1:5, NIV) "that if any of you lack *wisdom*, you should *ask God*, who gives generously to all without finding fault, and it will be given to you. I love those who love me, and those who *seek* me early shall find me."

Setting an example to be the first to love, the first to forgive offense, the first to show kindness and expressions of compassion and empathy, are giants as examples of godly leaders. It is not always easy, sometimes it is actually quite difficult. Regardless, allowing others to see the Christ that you teach or preach about in you can yield a profound effect. Sometimes, what we do speaks so loudly that others can barely hear our spoken words for having to watch our actions. What others observe from our example as leaders ought to be the outpouring of grace on display in enjoyable and in difficult times. These individual behaviors are examples of everyday men and women who choose to hold on to God's strength in love when leading others.

Problem Solving God's Way

To solve problems that arise among the membership, clearly both leaders and the people they serve must operate in submission to the Spirit and knowledge of knowing what God's Word says for handling concerns as they come their way.

The question church leaders should answer when challenges overwhelm operations including forms of worship in preaching, teaching and service, should be "WWJD - What would Jesus Do?"

Pastors and church leaders are confronted daily on multiple levels with trouble and discord. Sometimes issues come in the form of miscommunications or situational dilemmas rising from unresolved difficulties. Churches are filled with people who bring their own unique set of troubles or agendas to the assembly. Healthy spiritual churches find answers for many concerns, even the messy stuff occurring in the run of a day.

Keeping a focus on what would Jesus do to solve problems, several scriptures of problem-solving value are included in this topic. It is always first order that the church and members pray for guidance in working out solutions to issues that may hinder the smooth flow of equilibrium within the congregation. It is of utmost value that pastors and members maintain diligence with knowing what scripture says about problem solving God's way.

> Philippians 4:6 (ESV) - Do not be anxious about anything, but in everything by prayer and supplication with thanksgiving let your requests be made known to God.

> Proverbs 3:5 (ESV) - Trust in the LORD with all your heart, and do not lean on your own understanding.

> Matthew 18:15-18 (ESV) - If your brother sins against you go and tell him his fault, between you and him alone. If he listens to you, you have gained your brother. But if he does

not listen, take one or two others along with you, that every charge may be established by the evidence of two or three witnesses. If he refuses to listen to them, tell it to the church. And if he refuses to listen even to the church, let him be to you as a Gentile and a tax collector. Truly, I say to you, whatever you bind on earth shall be bound in heaven, and whatever you loose on earth shall be loosed in heaven.

Proverbs 3:6 (ESV) - In all your ways acknowledge him, and he will make straight your paths.

Psalm 50:15 (ESV) - And call upon me in the day of trouble; I will deliver you, and you shall glorify me.

Mark 11:22-25 (ESV) - And Jesus answered them, "Have faith in God. Truly, I say to you, whoever says to this mountain, 'Be taken up and thrown into the sea,' and does not doubt in his heart, but believes that what he says will come to pass, it will be done for him. Therefore, I tell you, whatever you ask in prayer, believe that you have received it, and it will be yours. And whenever you stand praying, forgive, if you have anything against anyone, so that your Father also who is in heaven may forgive you your trespasses.

1 John 1:9 (ESV) - If we confess our sins, he is faithful and just to forgive us our sins and to cleanse us from all unrighteousness.

Luke 17:3-4 (**ESV**) - Pay attention to yourselves! If your brother sins, rebuke him, and if he repents, forgive him, and if he sins against you seven times in the day, and turns to you seven times, saying, 'I repent,' you must forgive him.

1 John 4:19 (ESV) - We love because he first loved us.

James 5:16 (ESV) - Therefore, confess your sins to one another and pray for one another, that you may be healed. The prayer of a righteous person has great power as it is working.

2 Timothy 3:16 (ESV) - All scripture is breathed out by God and profitable for teaching, for reproof, for correction, and for training in righteousness.

Solving problems in the church requires members to be aware of the needs, anxieties, and even the crises of others who serve near and around them. Knowing specific details of issues or personal difficulties should not become a prerequisite to give support when needed. Wise approaches to change in conduct or disorder begin by seeking divine guidance to shaping effective communication with all connected to an issue. Relationship building is a genuine first step effort to solving issues and bridging fellowship for some problems in the church. Taking opportunity to get to know members on a personal basis is foundational to sharing meaningful life experiences of mutual respect with others. Sincere efforts to operate near this level of communication lessen the opportunity for discord or anxiety about perceived outcomes.

In his book, *Facing Messy Stuff in the Church: Case Studies for Pastors and Congregations,* Kenneth L. Swetland[49] reminds us of the time the Apostle Paul recognized the need for the Christians at Corinth to be sensitive to the many issues raised in the church.

In that regard, an admonition the apostle taught is that we can actually live relatively stable lives by guarding ourselves from the temptation of diving too deeply into the many swamps caused by unnecessary situations.

"Praise be to the God and Father of our Lord Jesus Christ, the Father of compassion and the God of all comfort, who comforts us in all our troubles, so that we can comfort those in any trouble with the comfort we ourselves received from God. For just as the sufferings of Christ flow over into our lives, so also through Christ our comfort overflows." (2 Corinthians 1:3-5, NIV).

When adhering to the hope of God, Paul envisioned a fellowship of people who come together to worship God, serve Him in the world, and be agents of healing in the lives of broken people, even brokenness found in the Church.

The church is tasked with an obligation to remain on message with God's mission, the message for the purpose of Jesus. Results to keeping a hope in

Jesus lead the church to maintain a continuous focus on seeing Christ in all matters and through every challenge.

Replacing and Reproducing Leaders

A transitional focus in leadership planning is presented in the next several topics to relate to methods pastors and congregations can process the need for continuous training of new and serving leaders working in the church. Developing for leadership is an ongoing responsibility to find and keep good members who are willing to serve in the congregation. These persons, individuals commissioned by God under the leadership of appointed pastors, use their talents, experiences in Christian education, and their training in leadership to support the vision and work of ministry. Members who possess a readiness to grow in discipleship will identify as persons who also desire to share their love for Jesus with others.

The church opens opportunity to promote annual training and recruitment to find and enlist help from the next generation of servants God will assign to connect to the call, vision, and mission of ministry for the congregation and with the community. The process for developing and sending disciples into the vineyard for service encourages people to identify with what God has called them to accomplish for the kingdom. Most people seated within the pews of every church do not give much thought to stepping out and leading others. Truthfully, some probably are not aware that they even possess skills to lead or direct in ministry. The following groups of texts can help pastors and experienced leaders track the gospel to prepare others for leadership service. The scriptures referenced here are support for potential leaders to see what God already knows exists in them if they are willing to expand their reach to grow.

Tracking the Gospels to Prepare Leaders

An excellent example for replacing and reproducing leaders for discipleship is found in Ephesians 4:11-16, (KJV), commonly referred to as the chapter for *Equipping the Saints for Service,* found in the New Testament. Greater attention to a fuller discussion on the importance of this reference will be presented in Chapter Seven. To equip people for transformational service was one of the apostle's greatest desires for the church. In his revelation, he describes how teaching the gospel moves Christians to a place of *actualization of the gospel message in a way that advances church maturity through discipleship.*

If a church desires to learn and adopt skills for finding and developing leaders, scripture identifies plans that Jesus the Master Teacher utilized with choosing and training his disciples for work in the kingdom.

Soon after His baptism by John the Baptist in the Jordan River, Jesus chose his first disciples. Sources of scripture present the *why* and the *how* of the Master's calling (Matthew 4: 18-22; Matthew 10:2-4; Mark 3:13-19; Luke 5:1-11; Luke 6:12-16). From the very first followers, he chose special men and appointed them to lead His church and bear witness, in due time, as apostles, of His resurrection.

Note the following importance placed on their personal revelations of Christ originating from the circumstances of their individual callings. Each of these gospel apostles wrote to report what they saw and heard from their unique personal perspectives. *Their Synoptic writings were consumed with the telling of their Christ as they came to know him.* Matthew, Mark, and Luke present Christ to tell of the major leader influences they felt from him. They told of learning from His teachings in salvation, deliverance and service. Follow their gospels to learn what they saw and how they interpreted His authority from four categories of identifications of Him: <u>*He Calls.*</u> <u>*He Selects.*</u> <u>*He Names.*</u> <u>*He Appoints.*</u>

1. Matthew - <u>*Jesus Calls the First Disciples:*</u> While walking the by Sea of Galilee as found in Matthew 4:18-22, ESV).

    "While walking by the Sea of Galilee, he saw two brothers, Simon (who is called Peter) and Andrew his brother, casting a net into the sea, for they were fishermen. And he said to them, "Follow me, and I will make you fishers of men. Immediately they left their nets and followed him. And going on from there he saw two other brothers, James the son of Zebedee and John his brother, in the boat with Zebedee their father, mending their nets, and he called them. Immediately they left the boat and their father and followed him." (<u>Matthew 4:18–22</u>, ESV).

2. Matthew - <u>*Jesus Names His Twelve Disciples*</u> (Matthew 10:2-4, ESV).

    [2] The names of the twelve Apostles are these: first, Simon, who is called Peter, and Andrew his brother; James the son of Zebedee, and John his brother;

³ Philip and Bartholomew; Thomas and Matthew the tax collector; James the son of Alphaeus, and Thaddaeus;

⁴ Simon the Zealot and Judas Iscariot, who betrayed him.

3.   Mark - *Jesus Appoints* the Twelve Apostles (Mark 3:13-19, ESV)

¹³ And he went up on the mountain and called to him those whom he desired, and they came to him.

¹⁴ And he appointed twelve (whom he also named Apostles) so that they might be with him and he might send them out to preach

¹⁵ and have authority to cast out demons.

¹⁶ He appointed the twelve: Simon (to whom he gave the name Peter);

¹⁷ James the son of Zebedee and John the brother of James (to whom he gave the name Boanerges, that is, Sons of Thunder);

¹⁸ Andrew, and Philip, and Bartholomew, and Matthew, and Thomas, and James the son of Alphaeus, and Thaddaeus, and Simon the Zealot;

¹⁹ and Judas Iscariot, who betrayed him.

4.   Luke - *Jesus Calls as the Crowd Pressed* in on Him (Luke 5:1-11, ESV)

"On one occasion, while the crowd was pressing in on him to hear the word of God, he was standing by "the lake of Gennesaret, and he was tow boats by the lake, but the fishermen had gone out of them and were washing their nets. Getting into one of the boats, which were Simon's, he asked him to put out a little from the land. And he sat down and taught the people from the boat.

And when he had finished speaking, he said to Simon. "Put out into the deep and let down your nets for a catch." And Simon answered, "Master, we toiled all night and took nothing! But at your word I will let down the nets." And when they had done this, "they enclosed a large number of fish, and their nets were breaking.

They signaled to their partners in the other boat to come and help them. And they came and filled both the boats, so that they began to sink. But when Simon Peter saw it, he fell down at Jesus' knees, saying, "Depart from me, for I am a sinful man, O Lord." For he and all who were with him were astonished at the catch of fish that they had taken, and so also were James and John, sons of Zebedee, who were partners with Simon.

And Jesus said to Simon, "Do not be afraid, from now on you will be catch men." And when they had brought their boats to land, they left everything and followed him." (Luke 5:1-11, ESV).

5. Luke - *Jesus Selects His Twelve* after Spending a Night in Prayer (Luke 6:12-16, ESV).

After a night of prayer on a mountain, Jesus called His followers together and formally chose twelve from among them to serve as His apostles:

When morning came, He called his disciples to Him and chose twelve of them, whom He also designated Apostles: Simon (whom He named Peter), his brother Andrew, James, John, Philip, Bartholomew, Matthew, Thomas, James son of Alphaeus, Simon who was called the Zealot, Judas son of James (also known as Thaddaeus, the name that is used in Matthew and Mark), and Judas Iscariot, who became a traitor." (Luke 6:13–16, NIV).

Likewise, accounts of the calling of the disciples can also be found in Mark 1:16–20, Luke 5:2–11, and John 1:40–42.

The amazing points we find in these Gospel accounts are that in each instance, when Jesus called the appointed follower, that person, whatever it was he had previously been involved in, left it and immediately followed Him. From that time on until the end of Christ's leadership with them, the disciples remained with Him to receive special training and hands on mentoring for a period of three years. For three years, they traveled with Him and witnessed His many miracles and were amazed by His teaching.

These men and also many women who faithfully followed Jesus to the end, studied from Him as He changed water into wine, healed the sick and paralytics, fed the 5000 and walked on water. Mary Magdalene, being the most notable of women who loved, followed, and learned from Jesus was among the women who were discipled by Him. What a powerful apprenticeship to follow; producing leaders from the hands-on power of the Almighty Himself. The same power of our Lord Christ is available to the church today. The holy anointing of God's Spirit is available to mentor members in leadership training for development as new leaders. God's love continues to grow leaders today as they remain faithful to the callings He has entrusted to them.

Reproducing Leaders in Simple Steps

As with all credible works in systems management, reproducing leaders for Christian service should follow an organized process in structure from start to finish. In his work, *"3 Simple Steps to Reproduce Church Leadership,"* Ron Edmonson, listed three simple ways to reproduce leaders in the church. His concluding message was that leadership training should produce disciples who love the work of the kingdom.[50] To reproduce leaders is to recruit them, develop them through training and release them to serve.

Recruiting requires that pastors and appointed team members actuate conversation to learn which spiritual gifts are present among the congregation. Assessing areas of interests and abilities from the membership can be conducted through surveys and focus group sessions with potential candidates engaged in recruiting for new leadership. Another factor in recruitment is to invite persons to shadow and model experienced leaders in their assigned church tasks. This hands-on recruiting tool is one that leads to new recruits seeing up close how leadership functions and how those who lead handle situations resulting from their responses.

Edmonson's *Ten Ways to Developing a Culture of Recruitment*[51] presents methods to create opportunity to systematically design assessment. The process includes identifying areas where the church prepares to plan, pursue, engage, train, and deliver quality leaders for service in leadership training.

Training in service is an excellent equipping tool that goes beyond the delivery of facts and knowledge for the work. Training actually provides step by step details for how to carry out the allocated service assignments. This level of preparation goes further than the teaching of details and concepts. To train is to provide guidance and exercises for working through what is being taught in a way that brings glory to the service of God for kingdom living. Investing in professional tools and resources necessary to training members in the way of leadership is also helpful.

Recruiting and training church members to embrace leadership qualities in preparation to respond to a calling is essential to each ministry. *However, a member has to be released for duty from a personal commitment of obedience to serve in ministry.* Usually, the pastor is the person to announce that a member has been released to conduct work in the congregation. Factors such as the nature and scope of responsibility of the leading role, how much time is involved in carry out the responsibilities, others who will serve with the newly released member are of immediate consideration. Family concerns and available resources necessary to manage the task should also be included with any release process.

Loving Christ and living to work as a leader motivated to follow the example of our Lord, requires continuous transformation of will and mind. Constant study in scripture, training in administrative, leadership, and managerial services are all necessary prerequisites to advancing quality service. The kingdom of God is in dire need of workers, persons who know the why and the how of service to the kingdom.

Actually, the *why* is so important, that the church cannot afford to just train for service; the church must equip hearts that love God. The church must be determined to place persons who are willing to sacrifice daily for the cause of the greatest love for humanity. This evolves from love for helping to build a church that grows from the heart of Christ. The church has many workers; what is necessary is more kingdom movers and dedicated servants who give real transformational service from the heart.

Follow the Master's Plan

The concluding message for Chapter Six provides details for how leadership transforms the church by encouraging pastors and leaders to follow the Master's plan. The greatest prototype for any church is the example Jesus gave to *present* and *produce* disciples to the world.

Healthy leadership reproduction leads to ministry expansion where leaders are proactive and intentional in their zeal to invest in the needs of their people.[52] Presenting a rather unselfish way of furthering the gospel message through *the reproduction method*, Adkins speaks of looking at the big picture through "long term investment and giving away the responsibility of ministry to others." In this regard, pastors and ministry leaders develop ways to equip their successors. He calls this the "transfer of responsibility method of training leaders."

Persons who lead at this level of development for discipleship see all leadership roles as interim roles.[53] They create a *succession to replace when needed* frame of reference at every level of leadership. Continuity in leadership is their greatest asset. There is little value for selfishness when leaders train from the heart of Jesus. He exemplified the ultimate example of laying aside all that one would consider valuable and important to follow the will of His Father.

Twelve purposeful methods churches should use to plan in ministry and to train their leaders are presented below. The list, although inconclusive in scope and content, follows the Master's plan for discipleship training in both service and leadership. They are a substantial listing accumulated from many years of service and observing leadership and management roles in the church and the community. The guiding foundation for the inclusion of each method is supported from scripture and study in the life and ministry of Jesus Christ. The list bears witness to experiences gained from personal years growing in ministry. It is an encouragement that church congregations adhere to including these methods to their protocols of annual planning in leadership:

> - Pray and seek God's spiritual guidance.
> - Pray with current leadership team members.
> - Develop a plan and devise strategies.
> - Teach the purpose and mission of discipleship for your church.
> - Disciple year round with a focus to produce purpose driven leaders.
> - Keep the church informed.
> - Be vigilant to build a personal and congregational commitment.
> - Announce new positions.
> - Share the vision of church growth.
> - Pursue teaching and training.
> - Simplify and bring clarity to the process.
> - Teach and model skills leading to servant and transformational leadership.

❖

CHAPTER SEVEN

Servant Leaders are Transformational Leaders

Biblical Mandate for Servant Leadership

Pastors and church leaders support the position that leading from a servant's heart is bedrock to the foundational truths of their ministries. Without question, our Lord led "to give His life as a ransom for many (Mark 10:45, NIV)." Likewise, Christian leaders who operate in business organizations and community ministries should also seek the delicate balance between providing excellent service to their constituents, while they make critical decisions to lead for the greater good in organizational change with profitability. In church organizations, the profit is adding saved souls to the church for the maturing of these saints who provide committed service to transform the kingdom.

The concept that leaders should classify themselves as either being a servant leader or a transformational leader, may not express the full meaning behind Christ's message to seek and "to save that which was lost" (Matthew 18:11, KJV). The Bible identifies that the finished work of Christ results in Christians who develop from both leadership styles; persons who love Christ, serve humanity, and participate in transforming the world around them. The transformation is viewed as converting others for Christ. Therefore, servant leaders develop followers who help the pastor produce churches where the membership is transformed to live from the heart of scripture; churches that will ultimately transform their communities for good.

Ed Stetzer and Tom Rainer put it best in their book, _Transformational Church_, when they wrote about churches that transform their culture by way of disciples who love the gospel and are committed to the works of the kingdom including worship, community, and mission.[54]

The Transformational Leadership of Jesus Christ

A Christ-like attitude, behavior, and submission from persons willing to do what pleases the Father had been shared by Jesus with His disciples in Matthew 20:22-25. Jesus had discerned that not only the sons of Zebedee desired fame and glory for their work, but perhaps all twelve of the disciples were guilty as well. Here is how Matthew's gospel summed the stance Jesus took with these disciples:

> "He said to them, "You will drink my cup, but to sit at my right hand and at my left is not mine to grant, but it is for those for whom it has been prepared by my Father." And when the ten heard it, they were indignant (greatly displeased) at the two brothers. But Jesus called them to Him and said, "You know that the rulers of the Gentiles lord it over them, and their great ones exercise authority over them. It shall not be so among you. But whoever would be great among you must be your servant" (Matthew 20:22-26, KJV).

The disciples had little idea that the high cost of leadership was going to be required of them to follow their Lord. The eye-opening reality was that they would in time live out the "die daily to self" (1 Corinthians 15:31, KJV) way of life and to "deny themselves by taking up their cross to follow Jesus (Matthew 16:24, KJV)." The Lord's wisdom-filled reprimand signaled His teaching the correct manner leaders must view their service in the kingdom. False ambition, vain glory, and self-centered motives prevent leaders from the true purpose for real and impending suffering and sacrifice on behalf of others.

Our Lord knew His cup was a bitter drink of surrender. Ministry to achieve measures of personal greatness is likened to officials of governments; persons who request honor and maintain dominion over others. This is the exact opposite of ministry from the mission of Christ. A keen sense of humility wrapped daily in prayer, seeking God's favor and grace from His Holy Spirit are established behaviors of all who lead or minister in the name of our Lord Christ. Because Christ came to save the lost, His mandate to follow ship was likewise, "whoever would be great among you must also be your servant" (Matthew 20:26, ESV).

Scripture teaches of the rewards to living the servant's life. Leading others from a heart filled with humility and obedience will be one that submits overwhelmingly to producing for good on behalf of Christ and His mission.

> "But whoever drinks of the water that I will give him will never be thirsty again. The water that I will give him will become in him a spring of water welling up to eternal life" (John 4:14, ESV).

This illustration of the conversation Jesus had with the Samaritan woman at the well is an example of Christ's lessons to teach the benefit of a life transformed by the Spirit. He associated this new life as one existing from a fountain of *living water* indwelling within us; filling our hearts and our wills to be transformed to the nature and character of Christ. This new fountain is called the Gift from the Source of all life, Christ Himself. By the gift of salvation, new life springs forth with an opportunity to never thirst again, for it is the Spirit of the Lord who will reside in the hearts of all who believe and rest in Him.

The resulting benefits include possessing a heart from the fountain that springs forth into everlasting life. There is now joy in place of sorrow when in times past, the body and mind existed in distress. Christ's living water offers satisfaction and contentment for persons to move away from the pursuits of seeking worldly pleasures from life's existence, to accept His gifts of love and grace with hope.

This everlasting fountain of renewal is new life and joy in the Holy Spirit. It is a life transformed by the power of God unto salvation necessary for an earthly ministry and in life everlasting. Pastors preach and teach this great work of redemption from their pulpits and Bible study classes. Their sacrificial study to present Christ as redeemer leads to lives being transformed for great works unto the glory of God.

Servant Leadership Identified from Scripture[55]

Consider below how scripture identifies characteristics of Servant Leadership:

> Mark 10:45 (NIV) - For even the Son of Man came not to be served but to serve, and to give His life as a ransom for many.

- ➤ 1 Peter 5:3 (ESV) - Not domineering over those in your charge, but being examples to the flock.
- ➤ John 13:12-15 (ESV) – When He had washed their feet and put on his outer garments and resumed his place, he said to them, "Do you understand what I have done to you? You call me Teacher and Lord, and you are right, for so I am. If I then, your Lord and Teacher, have washed your feet, you also ought to wash one another's feet. For I have given you an example, that you also should do just as I have done to you.
- ➤ Luke 22:26 (ESV) – But not so with you. Rather, let the greatest among you become as the youngest, and the leader as one who serves.
- ➤ Acts 20:35 (ESV) – In all things I have shown you that by working hard in this way we must help the weak and remember the words of the Lord Jesus, how He himself said, 'It is more blessed to give than to receive.'
- ➤ Hebrews 13:7 (ESV) - Remember your leaders, those who spoke to you the word of God. Consider the outcome of their way of life, and imitate their faith.
- ➤ Philippians 2:3-8 (ESV) – Do nothing from selfish ambition or conceit, but in humility count others more significant than yourselves. Let each of you look not only to his own interests, but also to the interests of others. Have this mind among yourselves, which is yours in Christ Jesus, who, though He was in the form of God, did not count equality with God a thing to be grasped, but made Himself nothing, taking the form of a servant, being born in the likeness of men.
- ➤ Acts 20:28 (ESV) - Pay careful attention to yourselves and to all the flock, in which the Holy Spirit has made you overseers, to care for the church of God, which He obtained with His own blood.
- ➤ Matthew 20:26 (ESV) - It shall not be so among you. But whoever would be great among you must be your servant.
- ➤ Matthew 20:28 (ESV) - Even as the Son of Man came not to be served but to serve, and to give His life as a ransom for many.
- ➤ Galatians 6:9 (ESV) - And let us not grow weary of doing good, for in due season we will reap, if we do not give up.
- ➤ Hebrews 13:17 (ESV) - Obey your leaders and submit to them, for they are keeping watch over your souls, as those who will have to give an account. Let them do this with joy and not with groaning, for that would be of no advantage to you.

Defining Servant Leadership

Servant leadership is an idea where the primary objective of the leader is to serve. Servant leadership dates back to the start of the Early New Testament Church and the advent of the ministry of Jesus Christ. The view of servant leadership is a timeless belief. It is leading with a heart to minister to the needs of others and the desire to bring about results to benefit even the least of those in the congregation. Servant leadership is the benchmark from which pastors and leaders emerge for good works. When Christ washed the feet of His disciples (John 13:12-15, ESV), He knelt to express lowliness of heart and to set an example to do for others as one desires for others to do for them.

Often people seek the position of leader with little to no concept of the sacrifice necessary for the position. It is with humility that leaders should present themselves on behalf of Christ for others. Leaders bear the responsibility to present Christ in words and deed; "although He was in the form of God, He made himself nothing, but took on the form of a servant (Philippians 2:3-8, ESV)."

Our Lord's first words in ministry began with His reading of the Old Testament scroll from the text of Isaiah. It was there, in the synagogue that Jesus acknowledged:

> "The Spirit of the Lord is upon Me, Because He has anointed me to preach the gospel to the poor, He has sent me to heal the brokenhearted, to proclaim liberty to the captives and recovery of sight to the blind, to set at liberty those who are oppressed," (Luke 4:18, KJV).

God sent His only Son to heal and to bring salvation to unjust men because of His love for the world.

The modern servant leadership movement began when Robert K. Greenleaf wrote his classic essay in 1970, *The Servant as Leader*. Greenleaf described the leader as someone who served. He coined the phrase "servant-leader" and thusly, the term servant leadership is used quite extensively today. Greenleaf's position on servant leadership was that "the servant-leader is servant first and begins with the position that one wants to serve; to serve first.[56]

The concept of servant-first is the trademark of the Servant Leader Model. To embrace servant leadership is to first serve, where leading becomes secondary to developing people. At its core is helping and caring for those within the group. Practices in servant leadership take into consideration all those *"shadings and blends of infinite variety of human nature."* [57]

An article from *Proofhub.com*, "7 Leadership Styles: Which Type of a Leader are You?" [58] presents insight for pastors and leaders to think about the particular ways they lead and manage the people they serve. While there are dozens of leadership styles available, the author considered seven to assist leaders with a focus on personality types. Personality characteristics relate to how a leader responds to outcomes and behaviors of others, which can evolve from their own personal leadership style.

The article goes on to say that *"leadership is not a position or a title, it is action and example" (Unknown).* The focus is that leadership is an extension of the leader's personality. Servant leadership is about having the right attitude to communicate the complexity of goals common to the completion of ministry for the organization. The following quote is this author's thoughts for what servant leadership means to the pastor as the leader and also for the people they serve.

> "A pastor is a faithful servant to his Master, the Lord Christ, the Chief Cornerstone of the church, to obediently receive divine wisdom and guidance to follow Christ. As a good shepherd, a pastor takes oversight to care for and provide for the spiritual needs of the people he or she has been appointed to lead and serve."

The pastor as servant leader adheres to 1 Peter 5:1-11 (KJV), *to "feed the flock of God which is among you and to take the oversight thereof."* This is one of the leading scripture passages specific to the work of pastors. The following is the NKJV translation of the scripture. Careful study of the text renews respect and appreciation for pastors, God's servant leaders for His church.

Shepherd the Flock

> "The elders who are among you I exhort, I who am a fellow elder and a witness of the sufferings of Christ, and also a partaker of the glory that will be revealed:
>
> [2] Shepherd the flock of God which is among you, serving as overseers, not by compulsion but willingly, not for dishonest gain but eagerly;

³ nor as being lords over those entrusted to you, but being examples to the flock;

⁴ and when the Chief Shepherd appears, you will receive the crown of glory that does not fade away. Submit to God, Resist the Devil

⁵ Likewise you younger people, submit yourselves to your elders. Yes, all of you be submissive to one another, and be clothed with humility, for "God resists the proud, but gives grace to the humble."

⁶ Therefore humble yourselves under the mighty hand of God, that He may exalt you in due time, ⁷ casting all your cares upon Him, for He cares for you.

⁸ Be sober, be vigilant; because your adversary the devil walks about like a roaring lion, seeking whom he may devour. ⁹ Resist him, steadfast in the faith, knowing that the same sufferings are experienced by your brotherhood in the world.

¹⁰ But may the God of all grace, who called us to His eternal glory by Christ Jesus, after you have suffered a while, perfect, establish, strengthen, and settle you.

¹¹ To Him be the glory and the dominion forever and ever." Amen. (1 Peter 5:1-11, NKJV)

Servant leader pastors look forward to that day when after they have suffered a while with the people of God, that the Great Shepherd of the Most High will perfect, establish, strengthen, and settle each one for His eternal glory!

Defining Transformational Leadership

Constructing a narrative for transformational leadership starts with a refocus on Christ's mandate to find and make disciples who mature in both character and conduct. The investment from the labor of transformational leaders is that members become equipped for service to others. Transformational leadership grows an organization, a business, a church, and even a community to seek its highest potential in mission and substance. Transformational leaders design objectives for their organizations by connecting *purpose* and *objectives* to their followers. The basic outcomes are to inspire and develop people who will move to the next level of mission engagement and commitment. Transformational leadership is generally activated by leaders who inspire others to move forward in the group with a high sense of commitment to visionary outcomes.

Transformational leaders focus on defining the mission, vision, and purpose of the organization to the membership via clear and straightforward methods of presentation. Transformational leaders challenge the organization to continuous growth by sharpening maturity for individual skills. They are good listeners who do not seek to evaluate every singular situation for their advantage. Rather, they encourage members within the group to keep going by giving them the confidence to never retreat, but to keep moving forward. Transformational leadership is leading with a determination to maintain focus for the core values of the organization.

These leaders understand and communicate God's purpose for the church with great detail and passion. They know that the church exists for the mission of God. Their target agenda is to guide persons who are without hope into a right relationship with Christ. Transformational leadership is the standard pastors strive to maintain for leading members to a steadfast devotion to the one true purpose God prepared for His church. Churches privileged to have pastors who are transformational leaders will experience life in Christ where members grow in maturity with a pursuit toward mission for the participation of continued life in Christ.

A Life Transformed in the Spirit[59]

Scripture has been highlighted here to share references useful for learning and growing as a transformational leader:

> 2 Corinthians 3:18 (ESV) – And we all, with unveiled face, beholding the glory of the Lord, are being transformed into the same image from one degree of glory to another. For this comes from the Lord who is the Spirit.

> Romans 12:2 (ESV) – Do not be conformed to this world, but be transformed by the renewal of your mind, that by testing you may discern what is the will of God, what is good and acceptable and perfect.
> 2 Thessalonians 3:5 (ESV) - May the Lord direct your hearts to the love of God and to the steadfastness of Christ.
> Galatians 5:22-23 (ESV) – But the fruit of the Spirit is love, joy, peace, patience, kindness, goodness, faithfulness, gentleness, self-control; against such things there is no law.
> 1 Corinthians 1:10 (ESV) - I appeal to you, brothers, by the name of our Lord Jesus Christ, that all of you agree, and that there be no divisions among you, but that you be united in the same mind and the same judgment.
> Colossians 3:5 (ESV) – Put to death therefore what is earthly in you: sexual immorality, impurity, passion, evil desire, and covetousness, which is idolatry.
> Joel 2:13 (ESV) – And rend your hearts and not your garments. Return to the Lord your God, for he is gracious and merciful, slow to anger, and abounding in steadfast love; and he relents over disaster.
> Acts 3:19 (ESV) – Repent therefore, and turn back, that your sins may be blotted out.
> Acts 2:38 (ESV)   And Peter said to them, "Repent and be baptized every one of you in the name of Jesus Christ for the forgiveness of your sins, and you will receive the gift of the Holy Spirit.

The Process for Transformation - Ephesians 4:11-16 (KJV)

The Apostle Paul illustrated in the Epistle to the Ephesians, what has been described as the *Jesus Model* for teaching the church to live the message of spiritual maturity in Christ. Transformational churches develop ministry to embrace the mandates of Ephesians 4:11-16 (KJV); members commit to *"mature to the whole measure of the fullness of Christ."* The passage speaks directly to pastors and elders to establish sound doctrine for developing and nurturing the church in spiritual growth and to live in unity with Christ. Members are taught to strive in their faith and to stay on the pathway to maturity to the measure of Christ. Provisions to grow in spiritu-al gifts through deeper study in God's Word are primary to living the deeper calling to mature in all His ways.

Exposition to the text is provided to explain the levels of learning and growth in the "maturing the saints for service" process. Growing in Christ is a *process*. The objective to set the text under topical headings brings clarity to major actions and *outcomes of transformation* experienced during the *process of change*. The stages of maturity are readily observed for easy illustration and teaching of the concept.

A. God gives transforming gifts to called out leaders in the Body (Ephesians 4:11, KJV).

> And he gave some, apostles; and some, prophets; and some, evangelists; and some, pastors and teachers;

B. These gifts given to church leaders to equip saints for works of service (Ephesians 4:12, KJV) so that the body will grow in unity, maturity, and in the character of Christ. All members receive individual gifts but the leaders' (pastors as teachers) tasks are to take the oversight to "equip the saints for the work of ministry." The equipping is the teaching, training, mentoring, and serving process.

> "For the perfecting of the saints, for the work of the ministry, for the edifying of the body of Christ."

C. Church members become perfected; the saints are transformed to a place of maturity in unity and unto Christ-like character. This produces saints who are pleased to perform from what the Spirit has delivered unto them, including works of ministry for others. The work is led by the pastor-teacher. They model, teach and perfect the vision for all to see and know. Saints conduct the ministry. The church is serviced by saints who continue (in unity) to reach toward "the mark for the prize of the high calling of God (in their lives) which is from Jesus Christ." Their cry to the Lord is "Let us therefore, as many as be perfect, be thus minded; and if in anything ye be otherwise minded, God shall reveal even this unto you." (Philippians 3:14-15, KJV). This is the maturing of Christians in the knowledge of the Son of God for the kingdom of God is at hand.

> "Till we all come in the unity of the faith, and of the knowledge of the Son of God, unto a perfect man, unto the measure of the stature of the fullness of Christ."

D. When the Body is built through Word-centered teaching from pastor-teacher leaders, the church begins to walk (live) in the statue (the measure, the ability, the wisdom, the disposition, the character, the lifestyle) of mature men (believers); and not as babes. Becoming grounded in a firm foundation of expository teaching brings about clarity of purpose and a single focused mindset to build the house for the saving of God's kingdom. This is growing to the measure of the stature that only belongs to the fullness of Christ. When we are unified, when we are grounded in the Gospel, and when we speak the truth in love, as well as serving and helping each other mature, the church is built to the stature of Christ.

> [14]That we henceforth be no more children, tossed to and fro, and carried about with every wind of doctrine, by the sleight of men, and cunning craftiness, whereby they lie in wait to deceive;
> [15]But speaking the truth in love, may grow up into Him in all things, which is the head, even Christ:
> [16]From whom the whole body fitly joined together and compacted by that which every joint supplieth, according to the effectual working in the measure of every part, maketh increase of the body unto the edifying of itself in love. (Ephesians 4:11-16, KJV).

Jesus Christ is the pure message for the New Testament Church. He lived to give generations clear and convincing methods for leaders to follow and practice in the administration of their duties on behalf of the church. He taught that the church may know Him and live life reconciled to perfecting His holy will, daily.

CHAPTER EIGHT

Leadership Principles for Disciple-Making Initiatives

Promoting Purpose through Collaboration

Relationship building is the foundation to the plan of salvation and the road that leads to finding and establishing disciples. Scripture is rich with examples of how God achieved kingdom goals through fellowship, partnerships, and what is commonly known in today's climate of professional development as *teamwork*. From the creation event of the first Adam when God spoke to the Trinity and said "let us" make man (Genesis 1:26, KJV), to the redemptive work of God the Father, God the Son and God the Holy Spirit at Calvary, teamwork has been instrumental in growing and moving the kingdom of God in the world. God the Father combined the work of the Trinity, from the power of the Holy Spirit to the sacrificial giving of His Son on the cross, as the supreme act of Spiritual collaboration on behalf of fallen man. The Father delivered the Son, and with the power of the Holy Spirit, man is delivered from death unto eternal life with Him.

What did Christ proclaim as the purpose of the church and the reason why He was sent by the Father? Did He not proclaim to the listeners His purpose on earth as He read from the scroll in the synagogue? From Isaiah sixty-one, verse one, Christ read that "the Spirit of the Lord God is upon me; because the LORD hath anointed me to preach good tidings unto the meek; he has sent me to bind up the brokenhearted, to proclaim liberty to the captives, and the opening of the prison to them that are bound." (KJV) Christ's purpose was to bring forth the kingdom of God and to bear witness of His Glory. We know His story. He gave His life for all who would believe that He would fulfill all that He was sent to accomplish.

The purpose to deliver on the promises of the Savior must be intentional! It has to be thoughtful and deliberate in both content and scope. Far too many essential parts are packed into the effective delivery of ministry that saves the lost, brings hope to the poor and brokenhearted, and sets at liberty all persons made captive by the bondages of an ensnared life. A pastor's organizational plan begins by promoting the concept of healthy collaborative administration in the church with the purpose to accomplish for others knowledge of the single reason for the church's existence.

The movement to promote collaboration advances for all to learn the '*why*' as well as the '*how,*' the church teaches the message of the mission of God. At the very heart to carry out all valuable church goals is the understanding that "we know who we are." Of equal importance is the church's commitment to articulate that "we know what it is we do; that we understand why we are here."

While the first part of knowing "*who we are*" is basic to the high calling to make disciples, it is usually in the knowledge, or the lack of knowledge for "*how do we carry out what we know*" that causes great consternation for moving God's mission forward with clarity in content and messaging. This is the area where major obstacles occur to any perceived methods to embrace and achieve mission goals and objectives vital to church doctrine within a rooted reality of scripture.

A lack of vision for strategy and organizational planning can account for why many well-intended church ministries have been derailed from the continuous pursuit of their first love; to effectively move the membership to sincerely participate in kingdom change. Management in ministry organization is of equal value to church mission outcomes as is articulating its purpose. Powerful preaching and coordinated teaching in God's Word must be paired with intentional designs to link knowledge with thought for new character and conduct.

The work of Christ in the kingdom is consistent with shedding light on the difference between *God's mission* and the *mission of God's people*. As His people, we are ambassadors commissioned to see His purpose fulfilled in the lives of those who confess a belief in the redemptive power of His transforming love. It is a lifetime commitment on behalf of others with others to participate in actions where people's lives become filled with purpose.

Biblical Illustrations in Discipleship Training[60]

The biblical text is invaluable when collecting and sorting thoughts to promote theological principles to apply methods of collaboration in building the kingdom of God from within groups or teams. Consider the following:

> Ecclesiastes 4:9-12 (ESV) – Two are better than one, because they have a good reward for their toil; for if they fall, one will lift up his fellow. But woe to him who is alone when he falls and has not another to lift him up! Again, if two lie together, they keep warm, but how can one keep warm alone? And though a man might prevail against one who is alone, two will withstand him—a threefold cord is not quickly broken.

> Proverbs 27:17 (ESV) – Iron sharpens iron, and one man sharpens another.

> 1 Corinthians 12:20-25 (ESV) –As it is, there are many parts, yet one body. The eye cannot say to the hand, "I have no need of you," nor again the head to the feet, "I have no need of you." On the contrary, the parts of the body that seem to be weaker are indispensable, and on those parts of the body that we think less honorable we bestow the greater honor, and our unpresentable parts are treated with greater modesty, which our more presentable parts do not require. But God has composed the body, giving greater honor to the part that lacked it.

> Philippians 2:1-30 (ESV) – So if there is any encouragement in Christ, any comfort from love, any participation in the Spirit, any affection and sympathy, complete my joy by being of the same mind, having the same love, being in full accord and of one mind. Do nothing from rivalry or conceit, but in humility count others more significant than yourselves. Let each of you look not only to his own interests, but also to the interests of others. Have this mind among yourselves, which is yours in Christ Jesus.

Ephesians 4:16 (ESV) - From whom the whole body, joined and held together by every joint with which it is equipped, when each part is working properly, makes the body grow so that it builds itself up in love.

1 Corinthians 1:10 (ESV) – I appeal to you, brothers, by the name of our Lord Jesus Christ, that all of you agree, and that there be no divisions among you, but that you be united in the same mind and the same judgment.

Romans 15:5-6 (ESV) – May the God of endurance and encouragement grant you to live in such harmony with one another, in accord with Christ Jesus, that together you may with one voice glorify the God and Father of our Lord Jesus Christ.

1 Peter 4:10 (ESV) – As each has received a gift, use it to serve one another, as good stewards of God's varied grace.

Hebrews 10:24-25 (ESV) – And let us consider how to stir up one another to love and good works, not neglecting to meet together, as is the habit of some, but encouraging one another, and all the more as you see the Day drawing near.

Leadership for Discipleship: Contentment and Satisfaction for Purpose

Jesus's model of leadership was transformative. Serious discussions on principles and methods for growing disciples are derived from the study of His leadership style and strategies. Jesus taught His followers and modeled for them through training and sharing examples and parables. He knew why He came and was thusly motivated to reach all mankind with the truth to live a life of blessings and hope in purpose. His goal was that everyday men would gain new strength in finding value to living sacrificially for others. The disciples continued to shoulder the burden to carry the Good News message long after Jesus was no longer with them. The significance of the Word would extend far beyond the existence of the early apostles and their followers. From those early days to now and for all the ages to come, the love of God is exemplified by His Son who came to redeem the lost to eternal life. The church would take on the responsibility to carry out the mssion message. This is the central legacy of Matthew 28:19-20 (KJV), The Great Commission.

Living sacrificially with others and working in harmony for the good of all begins with a study in Hebrews 10:24-25 (ESV) that saints are to assemble together in love and fellowship. Good works and right relationships are the results of working together.

> "And let us consider how to stir up one another to love and good works, not neglecting to meet together, as is the habit of some, but encouraging one another, and all the more as you see the Day drawing near." (Hebrews 10:24-25, ESV).

The text asks that Christians unite in worship and service. The idea to respect the interests (Philippians 2:4, ESV) and motivations of others with similar goals and needs is necessary to achieve in Christ. Having things in common is good for strengthening one another in times of need. During times of testings and trials, bonds of friendship can be strengthened to aid in bringing about needed healing of the soul and the body. Equally important is the necessity to produce works of Grace for Christ. It is our sacred duty to meet together and to work together for worship and ministry obligations.

Forming bonds of true friendships and mutual respect with fellow Christians makes it easier to manifest genuine love and excitement as Christians go about duties for mission and purpose. Real worship, godly character, and development in the work of sharing the great gospel message in preparation for the Day to come are true by-products of meeting and coalescing one with the other. Uniting as one in Christ binds hearts together so that when one hurts, all members to some measure or degree suffer together.

For this cause, every action that leads congregations to full participation in the kingdom agenda results from a pursuit to intentionally transform membership from within the context of spiritual order for discipleship. Every engagement with one another becomes an assignment to the final *shared outcomes* essential for the good of the whole..

Solving Mission Matters: A Work for the Entire Church

The partnership between God and the people of God is to maintain daily devotion to His mission. Every facet of church administration is considerate of the needs of the whole assembly. Mission matters begin in operation with counsel from the pastor. Growing disciples is not a one-time fix, nor is it a new church program; but rather, building for mission must be purposefully woven into the fabric of church culture. It is a matter for the entire church. It cannot be a "pastor only" undertaking. The purpose *is* the *work* of the church. Discipleship training is the church engaged in labor to accomplish for Christ in the kingdom. In this regard, church mission is the call to action for *all hands on deck.*

> "Then Jesus went about all the cities and villages, teaching in their synagogues, preaching the gospel of the kingdom, and healing every sickness and every disease among the people. But when He saw the multitudes, He was moved with compassion for them, because they were weary and scattered, like sheep having no shepherd. Then He said to His disciples, "The harvest truly is plentiful, but the laborers are few. Therefore pray the Lord of the harvest to send out laborers into His harvest," (Matthew 9:35-38, KJV).

Matthew 9:35-38 (KJV) recounts an occasion when Jesus had encountered a multitude of people who at that time in their lives, were found to be people in desperate need. Upon seeing them he spoke of them "as sheep without a shepherd." They required healing, they required guidance, and for many, deliverance. The text relates that Jesus was moved with compassion from what He saw. The empathy He felt as they drew closer to Him from every side moved Him with a grave sense of pity for the conditions of their circumstances. He immediately took the occasion to hand to his disciple's new insight for handling hardship as they encountered them. Jesus taught them how to participate with him in attending to the welfare of the crowds that followed them. Here was one of the many instances where the primary mission of the church rose to the top of the learning curve.

The connecting lesson Jesus taught was that meeting needs and seeking meaning through acts of helping others offered a fundamental process pattern to transform members for service. This is a view into the mind of Jesus regarding the scope, value, and purpose to *team lead, team train, and team serve.* The compassion of Jesus came from his realization that the people were *lost*! They were lost in so many ways and on multiple levels. They were not merely hungry. They did not just need a word of hope for deliverance. They came following him with as many needs as there were people. Verse thirty-five speaks of Jesus going about the duty to *"share the gospel, heal diseases, healing sufferings, hardships, and misery."* He answered huge and sobering problems on behalf of the crowd on that day.

Jesus had been teaching the Good News of God's kingdom and in many instances, He did so in the Jewish *churches* (the synagogues). Undoubtedly, religious leaders, scribes, priests, Levites, and Pharisees were in their place of service at these assemblies. Yet the people *STILL* wandered around, following Jesus and seeking the hope they felt from His words. From numerous causes, many Christians are wandering hopelessly today. They are looking for what may or may not be presented to them in their churches. Many church people are troubled in mind and many are hopeless in their knowledge of the healing power of the Savior. There are numerous reasons, for sure, why this reality exists; far too many to discuss in this subheading. Regardless, Jesus knew the problem and He had the answer! From His heart of mercy, He responded. His message to His disciples was that the crowd of followers is ready to believe. They were willing to obey and trust, but so few workers were available to help them. Few workers from among the many followers of Christ were equipped to bring the much-needed hope the crowd required for redemption.

His example that day: He simply stopped and addressed basic, in your face, necessities to set an example of the first order in leadership business; duties primarily targeted to the pastor of the church. This is the work of a shepherd. Jesus did what a shepherd does. There were so few workers to help the multitude of needs from the crowds of wanting people that Jesus admonished His disciples to pray. He said to them that they ought to first pray. He said they (the disciples, the leaders, His primary followers) must pray to God. They must pray to the Lord in charge of the Harvest, to ask Him to send more workers into His fields (Matthew 9:35-38, KJV). His message: Apostles, you must pray. Pray for God to send workers.

What a compelling message for the church today. Helping the pastor bring redemption in the congregation requires much-needed support from people in the church. Healing for the church requires help for the people. Deliverance in the church requires help to the people. Bringing hope to others in the church requires help with the people of God. What a revelation for God's people to know that the church must become equipped to do the work of the kingdom. God needs redeemed, delivered, hopeful saints to help hurting people. We are his disciples for today's wanting multitude. Pastors and anointed leaders operate under God's authority to accomplish every task imaginable within, and many, outside the church family.

The church, all of the people of God, is charged with the call to share the message of the Good News to everyone. How the church designs content and parameters of service to bring hope to the masses, will become that church's method to honor God's requirements to partner with Him in fulfilling His mission for Christ.

The church receives the mission. The church embraces the message. The church undertakes methods to become strengthened as genuine partakers to carry that hope to others. This is the mission of God for God's people. And yes, the church must continue to pray.

Model the Greatest Disciple-Maker

> "And Jesus came and said to them, "All authority in heaven and on earth has been given to me. Go therefore and make disciples of all nations, baptizing them in the name of the Father and of the Son and of the Holy Spirit, teaching them to observe all that I have commanded you. And behold, I am with you always, to the end of the age." (Matthew 28:18-20, KJV).

These final words of mandate to His eleven disciples, His apostles, were the foundation to a theology for worldwide mission to come. The mission from the cross was commissioned to the Jews first but also to Gentiles from far and near. The words of Jesus to His disciples before His ascension were His way of saying, *I now send you out.* They were to make disciples of all nations.

Christ's instruction to baptize and teach in the way of the Father was delivered to present the only pathway to salvation. All that the apostles learned while studying with the Master was now in their charge. They were at this time commissioned to take that knowledge to others. As a result of their obedience to the call, the masses would come to know the Messiah; the One who was crucified, and was now raised from the grave.

The disciples were commanded to instruct all persons they encountered with the doctrine of the Law, in obedience to truth, in love for mercy, and be persistent in faith. They were to teach all people from all nations and creeds to receive and follow all that Christ commanded. Christ's love and His abiding mercies would dwell with them richly, from the time He commissioned them, until now, and to the end of the age. Salvation was assured for all who received the Good News message and accepted it by faith.

For the sake of repetition, here, again, is a responsible place to state the mission of the church. The church is to "go and make disciples of all nations." The pattern left by the Lord has been outlined for today as it was in the days of the One for whom the church came into being. By the power and authority of Him who sends, the church goes. As a result of going, there is the command to make disciples.

1. Go and make disciples.
2. Baptize them in the name of the Father, Son, and Holy Spirit.
3. Instruct them in all the Lord has commanded.
4. Teach them to observe all that the Lord had commanded.
5. Know that the Lord would be with the church to the end of time.

A Culture of Church Growth

The mandate to "go and make disciples" is an emphatic command given as the purpose for why the church exists. Moving people from where they are without Christ, to where they live to exist in Christ is the transforming message of the New Testament's Great Commission.

Growing in the knowledge of the Lord Jesus is not an afterthought, nor is it an exercise in the delivery of special programs or special events occasions. Members must know and be able to articulate with a sense of clarity, what it is they expect to receive from their church affiliation. To grow in Christ and to become a catalyst of change for others is the *bend in the arch* for every church built on the Rock of Peter's confession of faith in his Savior. *This must be the nature and the culture of a church as it navigates saints toward disciplined Christian service.*

Just exactly how does a church *become a climate of disciplined service in the kingdom?* Listed below are questions church pastors and leadership team members ask of the proficiency of their church to clearly define and be able to share "what is the purpose for their hope in Christ."

1. How well do members know from day one that they are about to embark on a life-changing experience; a journey they will continue until the end of their life as a result of their faith?

2. How does a church combine strong doctrinal teaching in the faith with instructing members to strive to living daily the discipleship path of Christ?

3. Do pastors and leaders clarify the process of transformation in the church? On the contrary, do time and neglect force members to fill in the gaps on their own after hope from other life alternatives has been lost?

4. Where is the membership's understanding that they were redeemed for a cause; to live out a faithful life in service for others?

5. Do new members understand that their only purpose for membership is to grow in knowledge and unto the likeness of Jesus?

6. Is the declaration of obedience, to honor the one True and Living Savior, the first statement of promise asked of new Christian converts at the time of salvation or membership?

A clear understanding of the disciple-making process must become common conversation within the congregation. The pastor takes the lead to invest in teaching, profoundly sharing this message, daily. The climate and culture of a spiritually maturing church empowers new and seasoned members to live in victory and joy in the Lord. The message must be clearly identified early in their call to service.

Several authors are included in this section to add discus-sion for how churches can create a climate of continu-ous disciple-making training within the congregation. Key points from an article, *Essentials for Creating a Discipleship Making Culture in Your Church*[61] were presented by Philip Nation, along with authors Eric Geiger and Michael Kelley. These authors highlighted thought for the worthiness to create a continuous culture of disciple-making at all times in the life of the church.

In 2012, Phillip Nation[62] wrote responses from an interview process he had obtained on the subject of how to create a culture for growing in discipleship. Upon completion of the *Transformational Discipleship Project, Creating a Discipleship Making Culture,* Nation[63] interviewed, among others, two pastors who had made building a church around a culture of disciple-making a model for their congregations. These pastors were Steve Murrell[64] and Jon Ferguson.[65]

Both pastors shared inspiring ideas congregations can use to support their visions of designing sound cultures in a church that are built on duty to growing and sending disciples for service.

In a second appealing work, *"How to Grow a Disciple-Making Culture in Your Church," Godwin Sathianatha,* gave practical guidelines to define discipleship and to provide step-by-step procedures churches should follow to create a culture for disciple-making.[66]

Both models included in this disciple-making discussion, are referenced to stimulate further discussion for new and continuous ongoing conversations in engagement for church mission as it relates to developing a culture for the work.

Churches with active continuous disciple-making ministries produce followers who become aware of their own personal calling in the kingdom. Followers serving at this level of maturity eagerly share their knowledge with others. As a result, more members enlist their dedication to lead others to also obtain to the measure to the fullness of Christ. This path toward spiritual transformation helps to guide healthy growth for genuine authentic service within the congregation.

The Effective Team Design

Gathering together in the assembly is the first level of ministry alliance to work collaboratively in the church. As mentioned previously, one method to achieving common goals in the kingdom is through the mutually dependent function of working in teams. Teamwork has been defined as "the ability to work together toward a common vision. Teamwork is the fuel that allows common people to obtain uncommon results." [67]

Team leadership is about guidance. It is fulfilling the plans and purpose of God by establishing and working together in relationships. The outcomes of teamwork are far greater than results from solo performances. Teams achieve and endure to create success and long-term support. When the people of God work harmoniously toward the work of God, the Word of God is expanded to facilitate the needs of everyone.

> "A team is a group of people who are mutually dependent on one another to achieve a common goal." [68]

Leading is the complex alignment existing in relationships between people and those whose jobs are to see that the work of the assembly is carried out decently and in order. How many times should the obvious '*leadership is not easy*' be repeated? There are so many challenges to confront and equally as many barriers to overcome. Effective leaders mobilize their resources to recruit, produce, and develop the right workers for teams of excellence.

There are long-term advantages to selecting the right people, assigning the right work, and moving on to evaluate the work with adequate communication, data, and follow-up. The leader's purpose for organizational outcomes has to be as clear and compelling in teams as in general congregational service. Continuous repetition in instruction and guidance are necessary to establish the best direction a congregation should follow when setting in motion the ministry of discipleship with teams.

Vital questions leaders ask of themselves and the team members they recruit are "How do we bring others into the space to embrace the mindset of this culture's discipleship methodology?" and "What are the strategies best suited for our particular membership?" An important point here is to create an environment where people will want to be a part of a movement that impacts lives to make a positive difference.

Transitioning from a traditional service model to advance new endeavors and models for ministry in the church should flow within the present operating systems for a smooth, Spirit-led approach to change. Roll out to the church body the news of discipleship training, the disciple-making curriculum, and new disciple enhanced enrichments with new strategies. Share the scope and description of members of the organizational team. The impacting discipleship team design model has been created to support a church's position to move the entire congregation toward continuous ongoing discipleship training.

Impacting Discipleship for Leadership Training in Teams

1. Make the vision clear!
2. Send the message out with strength and sincerity. Use humility and the spirit of inclusion.
3. Allow everyone an opportunity to know and see where a vision for disciple-making will take the church to increased spiritual formation and growth.
4. Give ideas for evaluating the outcomes at the time objectives that are presented. People like ideas where they think they will realize results.

The following diagram is useful to outline simple steps a pastor and church leaders can use to inform and recruit members from the congregation for specific discipleship training and working in teams for works of service.

<u>Bring them Aboard! Train them for Service! Release them to Work!</u>

Strategies for an invitation to members to serve on disciple-making Teams

Pray about the need and the required process
Recruit members to attend a discipleship strategy planning meeting
Send invitations to members to come, see and talk
Select the right people to assign to the right work
Communicate the work, bring clarity to the vision, give compelling directions
Assess the process. Evaluate the work. Review for follow-up.

As with all essential teaching and training in church growth to move the congregation from membership to discipleship, these strategies are pastor-led and member-focused. Leadership teams serve to enable success for disciple-making.

The Character of a Disciple-Making Team

As with the culture of the entire church, the personality of leadership teams is as effective as the nature and nurturing hearts of its leaders. The character of the lead pastor paired with the spiritual maturity of appointed team members will be equal to the spiritual outcomes of proposals and projects initiated by church leaders and the persons selected to serve.

Look carefully at each category of personality characteristics to assist your church in measuring the plum line of alignments for team-building efforts. Always consider the relationship that exists between the nature of the church and the love and mercy of Christ as He gave of Himself in service for others.

The Pastors' Character

1. Be apt to preach, teach, and lead.
2. Be submitted to the Call of Christ for the Mission of the church.

3. Love and possess the passion for study in God's Word.
4. Love to feed the flock of God for which you have oversight.
5. Be clothed with humility and grace.
6. Pray diligently for laborers for the vineyard.
7. Seek out the right people for the tasks at hand.
8. Establish the vision, collaborate the strategy, structure the process.
9. Intentionally make disciples who will be equipped for ministry.
10. Communicate! Communicate! Communicate!

Team Leaders' Character

1. Submit to the vision from the authority of the pastor.
2. Develop a heart for the work of the Great Commission.
3. Know your spiritual gifts and how their function in the body.
4. Learn the commission of your congregation.
5. Work from within the heart of the culture of your church.
6. Spend time praying, studying, and meditating in the Word.
7. Seek genuine relationships with others.
8. Refrain from pride, arrogance, and selfishness.
9. Live obediently to God's will for your life.
10. Develop a sense of responsibility to commitment.
11. Pray for those you shepherd or lead in your team.
12. Diligently guide your team members with compassion and love.
13. Study organizational skills for management as required.
14. Communicate with the pastor for directions and alignment of all systems.
15. Monitor and evaluate your work.
16. Allow the Holy Spirit to guide your decisions.

The entire church will grow fruitfully in the mission to spiritually present members for Christ when the leadership team embodies the rich characteristics of heart and soul. Training in equipping for ministry is vital. Do not neglect adequate training for service. Commit to living as a disciple as you seek to disciple others.

SECTION THREE

A Transformational Model for Administration

CHAPTER NINE

The Church and Ministry Administration

God's Called-Out Church

¹³ When Jesus came into the coasts of Caesarea Philippi, He asked His disciples, saying, Whom do men say that I the Son of man am?

¹⁴ And they said, Some say that thou art John the Baptist: some, Elias; and others, Jeremias, or one of the prophets.

¹⁵ He saith unto them, But whom say ye that I am?

¹⁶ And Simon Peter answered and said, Thou art the Christ, the Son of the living God.

¹⁷ And Jesus answered and said unto him, Blessed art thou, Simon Barjona: for flesh and blood hath not revealed it unto thee, but my Father which is in heaven.

¹⁸ And I say also unto thee, That thou art Peter, and upon this rock I will build my church; and the gates of hell shall not prevail against it.

¹⁹ And I will give unto thee the keys of the kingdom of heaven: and whatsoever thou shalt bind on earth shall be bound in heaven: and whatsoever thou shalt loose on earth shall be loosed in heaven. (Matthew 16:13-19, KJV)

Located within this passage from Matthew's gospel is the first time the word church (ecclesia) was named in the New Testament. Jesus had posed a question to His disciples first asking *"who did men say that He was?"* Most importantly He wanted to know who *"did they say He was."*

Having been men who had taken up their spiritual cross and followed Him for the past three years, Jesus wanted them to tell Him who they would say He was to them. Men, who had seen His miracles and witnessed His feeding the multitudes, healing the sick and even raising the dead, must surely be at a place where they could say that they "know Him." Men who would be the first to receive the keys to unlocking the gospel message of the kingdom of heaven had to surely acknowledge the One they would soon be left to preach and teach about as they tell His story to new generations of believers.

Simon Peter was the spokes person and the other disciples agreed, that *"thou art the Christ, the Son of the living God."* Upon hearing the confession of Peter's unwavering faith in Him; that Jesus was indeed the Christ, the true Messiah, the Holy One who was promised by God; at this point, Jesus was assured that He would indeed now build His church. The gospel mission was from this point being commissioned from Christ to His apostles and on to the world.

What is the Church?

There is probably not one person reading this book that has not made the statement from childhood to the present that "I am a member of a church or I am going to church, or I belong to a certain denominational church affiliation." These statements define the church as a building, an edifice, or a worship center to attend service and to meet God in worship at a given location. While the building is indeed expressed as a church, and thusly, the house of God, the place of worship to the Most High God, the church that Christ spoke about when He announced "I will build my church," is different from any building erected by man.

Local assemblies are churches defined by location with a pastor and assisting leadership elders serving to watch over the body of believers commonly known as the flock (1 Peter 5:1, NIV). These leaders have been charged with the oversight to feed, care for and nourish the believers in their charge. Therefore, local churches require congregational leadership whose responsibility is to provide overall guidance for the members of the body.

The church Christ spoke of is a gathering of people; persons who have received Him as Lord of their lives. As head of the body of believers who have been converted into the faith, Christ holds the keys to unlock the doors for all to receive Him. The gift of receiving Him carries the hope to enter in and become part of His body, which is His shed blood, and His redemption, as new believers in the faith.

From this perspective, the church is therefore not a building. It is described in the New Testament to identify the community of believers in Jesus Christ. It literally means "assembly," "congregation," or "meeting." Similar terms were used in the Old Testament referring to experiences such as "the day of the assembly" (Deuteronomy 18:16, NIV), "the congregation of the Lord" (Numbers 16:3, KJV), or "meeting before the Lord" (Exodus 29:42, ESV). The church has also been described as an organism because of the lifeblood connection with people serving God and relating as brothers and sisters to each other in the Holy Spirit.

Christ is the head and the church is the body of Christ (Ephesians 1:22-23, KJV). The members of the body are all Christians. "For just as the body is one and have many members, and all the members of the body, though many are one body; so it is with Christ. For in one Spirit we were all baptized into one body" (1 Corinthians 12:12-13, ESV).

Church Purpose and Ministry Administration

Understanding the purpose of the church and its need for excellent administration requires a short review of God's purpose for truth. As stated in the introduction of this book, *to know Christ is to trust His redeeming power* for all who would believe is God's mission for the church. The church exists only when it is *in mission with God*. God desires that the world may know Christ, His only Begotten Son. As our Lord delivered Christ to the redeemed, the church, His Ambassadors, join Him to carry Christ to the world. New converts in turn share in the glorious acts of redemption and discipleship.

But how does the church conduct the work of mission to accomplish all that has been assigned to its hands? How does the church bring administrative order to daily organizational operations while staying on Christ's message with the people who serve and those to whom the church is dedicated to give service? Regardless of the many complexities found in the operation of church administration, the ultimate destiny for man is to know Jesus. It is God's will that Christ will be exalted and that administrative management will be useful to the process in the church.

Church Purpose: The Administration of the Great Commission

The first example given to express His purpose for the church is the mandate from the Great Commission (Matthews 28:19-20, KJV). God sent the church to spread the Good News message to the world that lost sinners might be saved. All missional decrees are carried out in the name of the Father, the Son, and the Holy Spirit. First Peter 2:4-5 and 9-10, (KJV) explains that the birth of a fallen nation is delivered to become a chosen race, a royal priesthood and a people renewed for His own possession.

Church Purpose: The Excellencies of the Power of God toward Mankind

Secondly, the church proclaims the Excellencies of the One who called the lost out of darkness into His marvelous light. Leaders of faith working through the power of God's anointed grace, who are built up in this conviction, believe that if "there is any sick among the congregation, the elders are called upon to pray over them, anointing them with oil in the name of the Lord" (James 5:14, KJV). This forward work of confidence in glory builds up a spiritual house, one that consistently offers sacrifices acceptable to God through the redeemer, Jesus Christ.

Church Purpose: The Power of Worship among the Saints

A third example to express purpose for the church is found in its worship. The church worships God together with one another; encouraging each one in the faith, lifting songs and hymns of thanksgiving to a merciful Father who watches over His church because He cares. The church does not neglect the assembling together of saints, but rather exhorts one another, knowing that the day of His return (Hebrews 5:11, KJV) is at hand. For this cause, the church resolves to comfort one another and to edify (First Thessalonians 5:11, KJV) each other as a body of believers in the faith.

Church Purpose: The Edification of Teaching the Word of God

A fourth reality for the purpose of the church is in the edification of teaching. The church pursues a single-minded goal to become rich in teaching Christ to the point that the Word of God dwells in its members richly (Colossians 3:16, KJV). The Word of the Lord admonishes that the church devote itself to instruct in its doctrine, to fellowship with each other and to remember His death, burial and resurrection until He comes again (Acts 2:42, KJV). This faith-building teaching admonishes all to grow in wisdom with hope and knowledge that *"He who began a good work in you will carry it on to completion until the day of Jesus Christ* (Philippians 1:6, KJV). This is teaching that *"fills the heart with all joy and peace as you trust in Him to the point of overflowing hope by the power of the Holy Spirit"* (Romans 15:13, KJV).

Church Purpose: Spiritual Gifts at Work in the Congregation

The fifth, yet most compelling purpose for the church is the provision of leaders gifted in their crafts to preach, teach, and lead. Spiritual leaders equip the saints for the work of ministry that the body of Christ may grow to maturity. These persons include pastors who have been appointed to oversee the operation of this task for the church (Ephesians 4:11-12). When the church positions itself to grow in maturity before a mighty God, the wisdom of God is made known to rulers and authorities (Ephesians 3:10, ESV) in heavenly places. Heavens hears and spiritual blessings fall upon the works with wonders; all may view in amazement the power of God at work in the church.

The purpose of the church is to therefore experience the spiritual benefits God has afforded His family as believers in Christ Jesus. God wills that His operational gifts unfold within the body to teach, equip, care and reach all who come to know Him. No matter the size of a local church, the purpose is to do what all who call on the name of Jesus are to do individually—glorify God in worship, obey and honor Him in deeds, and encourage one another in the faith. The church finds purpose in fulfilling its God-ordained mission.

A Theology for Church Administration

As a system of organizational order, church administration carries relevance to the overall effectiveness of all outcomes for the church. Each facet of church administration can be traced from scripture, where the Word of God gives directives to administrative design and duty. It is in biblical research that church leaders gain insight for quality movement from *Scripture, to Vision, to Mission.* The church functions when goals for leadership, administration and the tools of management can be traced to what God has recorded and how effectively man obeys. Duties in obligations from pastors and anointed members are accomplished through study in His text. When church vision is aligned with organizational realities, principles for a theology of administration govern the heart of all systems arrangements and operational management.

A listing of administrative and managerial vocabulary has been compiled to aid in understanding this section. These vocabulary terms have generally been used to describe structures common to systems of organizations. The inspiration for this level of grouping is to *track* the essence of each vocabulary with its added value to church administration. The next thought is to then *relate* that value in administration to what God says about that particular reference within the purpose and scope of the church. The last effort is to *align* the vocabulary with the church's relationship to operations of administration for edification in management.

The four categories of vocabulary chosen have historically been associated with corporate administration and many systems found in business management. In the context of this volume and to illustrate relevance to operations for the church, these terms are grouped to reference how scripture can aid to help pastors, elders, and team leaders match the vision in systematic organizational reality to the power of the Word of God for carrying out the work of the church. The list is not exhaustive; rather it is limited to a few primary sources for this chapter.

Note carefully the alignment with scripture for each category of administrative functioning for work in church organizations.

1. *Vision, Leadership, Organizational Systems Management, Strategies –* Leadership and Management

> Titus 1:5 (ESV) – This is why I left you in Crete, so that you might put what remained into order, and appoint elders in every town as I directed you.

> 1 Corinthians 12:28 (ESV) – And God has appointed in the church first apostles, second prophets, third teachers, then miracles, then gifts of healing, helping, administrating, and various kinds of tongues.

> 1 Timothy 5:17 (ESV) – Let the elders who rule well be considered worthy of double honor, especially those who labor in preaching and teaching.

Ephesians 4:11 (ESV) – And he gave the apostles, the prophets, the evangelists, the shepherds and teachers.

1 Corinthians 12:28-31 (ESV) – And God has appointed in the church first apostles, second prophets, third teachers, then miracles, then gifts of healing, helping, administrating, and various kinds of tongues. Are all apostles? Are all prophets? Are all teachers? Do all work miracles? Do all possess gifts of healing? Do all speak with tongues? Do all interpret? But earnestly desire the higher gifts. And I will show you a still more excellent way.

1 Timothy 3:2 (ESV) – Therefore an overseer must be above reproach, the husband of one wife, sober-minded, self-controlled, respectable, hospitable, and able to teach.

1 Peter 5:1-4 (ESV) – So I exhort the elders among you, as a fellow elder and a witness of the sufferings of Christ, as well as a partaker in the glory that is going to be revealed: shepherd the flock of God that is among you, exercising oversight, not under compulsion, but willingly, as God would have you; not for shameful gain, but eagerly; not domineering over those in your charge, but being examples to the flock. And when the chief Shepherd appears, you will receive the unfading crown of glory.

Ephesians 3:9 (ESV) – And to bring to light for everyone what is the plan of the mystery hidden for ages in God who created all things.

Acts 13:1 (ESV) – Now there were in the church at Antioch prophets and teachers, Barnabas, Simeon who was called Niger, Lucius of Cyrene, Manaen a member of the court of Herod the tetrarch, and Saul.

2. *Ministry, Teaching/ Training/Mentoring, Priorities on People* –Leadership, Administration, and Management

Acts 6:1-15 (ESV) – Now in these days when the disciples were increasing in number, a complaint by the Hellenists arose against the Hebrews because their widows were being neglected in the daily distribution. And the twelve summoned the full number of the disciples and said, "It is not right that we should give up preaching the word of God to serve tables. Therefore, brothers, pick out from among you seven men of good repute, full of the Spirit and of wisdom, whom we will appoint to this duty. But we will devote ourselves to prayer and to the ministry of the word." And what they said pleased the whole gathering, and they chose Stephen, a man full of faith and of the Holy Spirit, and Philip, and Prochorus, and Nicanor, and Timon, and Parmenas, and Nicolaus, a proselyte of Antioch.

2 Timothy 3:16-17 (ESV) - All scripture is breathed out by God and profitable for teaching, for reproof, for correction, and for training in righteousness, that the man of God may be competent, equipped for every good work.

1 Corinthians 12:5 (ESV) – And there are varieties of service, but the same Lord.

Romans 12:8 ESV) – The one who exhorts, in his exhortation; the one who contributes, in generosity; the one who leads, with zeal; the one who does acts of mercy, with cheerfulness.

Isaiah 41:10 (ESV) – Fear not, for I am with you; be not dismayed, for I am your God; I will strengthen you, I will help you, I will uphold you with my righteous right hand.

1 Corinthians 12:1-31 (ESV) - Concerning spiritual gifts, brothers, I do not want you to be uninformed. You know that when you were pagans you were led astray to mute idols, however you were led. Therefore I want you to understand that no one speaking in the Spirit of God ever says "Jesus is accursed!" and no one can say "Jesus is Lord" except in the

Holy Spirit. Now there are varieties of gifts, but the same Spirit; and there are varieties of service, but the same Lord.

3. *Service Model, Decision Making, Teams, Procedures* – Leadership, Administration, and Management

> Deuteronomy 28:1-68 (ESV) - And if you faithfully obey the voice of the LORD your God, being careful to do all his commandments that I command you today, the LORD your God will set you high above all the nations of the earth. And all these blessings shall come upon you and overtake you, if you obey the voice of the LORD your God. Blessed shall you be in the city, and blessed shall you be in the field. Blessed shall be the fruit of your womb and the fruit of your ground and the fruit of your cattle, the increase of your herds and the young of your flock. Blessed shall be your basket and your kneading bowl.

> 1 Corinthians 14:40 (ESV) – But all things should be done decently and in order.

> Romans 12:8 (ESV) – The one who exhorts, in his exhortation; the one who contributes, in generosity; the one who leads, with zeal; the one who does acts of mercy, with cheerfulness.

> Romans 8:28 (ESV) – And we know that for those who love God all things work together for good, for those who are called according to his purpose.

4. *Responsibilities, Staff Duties* – Leadership, Administration, and Management

> Deuteronomy 28:47-48 (ESV) – Because you did not serve the LORD your God with joyfulness and gladness of heart, because of the abundance of all things, therefore you shall serve your enemies whom the LORD will send against you, in hunger and thirst, in nakedness, and lacking everything. And he will put a yoke of iron on your neck until he has destroyed you.

Hebrews 13:17 (ESV) – Obey your leaders and submit to them, for they are keeping watch over your souls, as those who will have to give an account. Let them do this with joy and not with groaning, for that would be of no advantage to you.

Romans 13:4 (ESV) – For he is God's servant for your good. But if you do wrong, be afraid, for he does not bear the sword in vain. For he is the servant of God, an avenger who carries out God's wrath on the wrongdoer.

Administrative structure is useless without the skills of well-trained and organized administrators working with vision to see it through. These called out and assigned individuals are the pastors, church leaders, office managers, and team members who make it a priority to ensure the daily efficiency of all organizational structures. People resources, members and all persons associated with the church will achieve the benefit of kingdom outcomes for church objectives when knowledge and procedures are managed from within a system of spiritually task-oriented order.

Pastors, ministry leaders, and elders (matured leaders of the church and persons who work closely and in corporation with the pastor) are support to team members. These persons may include paid and volunteer staff, office administrative assistants, and all who make up the administrative services and appointments in the church.

Excellence in Administration

The local church as an assembly of believers is an equipping operation with tremendous moving parts. Every ministerial component of the church operates from objectives necessary for the church to accomplish spiritual goals for all believers in areas of worship, obedience and glorifying God through service. Amid spiritual matters, there are also all things practical, purposeful and systematic.

As with all organizational structures, the church operates within the scope of management by leadership. The call to great work requires church administration that prepares leaders to function from a diversity of gifts, talents and professional abilities. From the expository and exegetical delivery of the preaching of the gospel, to the management of evangelism and leadership operations, the church transforms membership to discipleship by mandating that all things be done decently and in order. Rendering service for the poor and downtrodden in the community equally involves quality church administration to equip members with the fortitude to endure.

Effective church administration goes hand in hand with quality management of operations. While administration guides the plan for organizational strategies with vision and wisdom, management directs and oversees critical functions within the structures of organizational methodologies. Day-to-day principles of operation remain true to the values and practices for the mission of the church. The mission of God is that Christ is visible in all applications, grand or meager, which requires close adherence to theological beliefs for the congregation.

Administration is the force that plans and makes decisions for the church. Scripture is the guidepost that steers administrative thought and development. "What we Believe" is the driving force behind all exercises with the singular purpose to lead believers to a place of sacred worship, obedience in the Word, and a ready spirit to glorify God.

In the work, *Key Elements of an Effective Church Administration*,[69] a definition for church administration was given as follows:

> "Church Administration equips the church to be the church and to do the work of the church in a coherent and comprehensive manner. It is the guidance provided by church leaders as they lead the church to use its spiritual, human, physical, and financial resources to move the church toward reaching its objectives and fulfilling its purpose. Church Administration enables the people of God who make up the church to become and do what they can become and do, by God's grace." [70]

Elements critical to support quality church administration should include (1) the church's overarching concern to fulfill the purposes of God; the understanding that (2) church administration is comprehensive in light of many tasks to perform in the church; and (3) in some way, all members of the church are engaged in administrative responsibilities.

Leadership in Church Administration

Directing and leading are invaluable components to the office of the pastorate. The pastor is required by God to be a leader/administrator. God gives the pastor to a church to prepare believers to minister and build up the body of Christ (Ephesians 4:11, KJV). In other words, the pastor is not only ordained to work with the congregation but he is also ordained to teach the congregation *to work*.

It is not the Master's plan that churchgoers come to worship to just sit in service; but rather all are to take up their personal cross as followers of Christ. A pastor's ability to adequately disperse leadership through skills and administrative tools to prepare the church for engagement in the mission of God, leads the church towards a life of spiritual transformation. As presented from Chapter Five, these tasks are inclusive of God's ordained responsibilities for the pastor.

How that responsibility fits into the administrative tier of pastoral duties can be traced to three basic prerequisites major to the work of the pastor. We know them as (1) preaching and teaching the Word (1Timothy 4:13), (2) leading the people by taking the "oversight thereof" (1 Peter 5:2, KJV), and (3) shepherding members with loving care (1Peter 5:1). Because the Holy Spirit has placed pastors in the church to look over and watch after members of a local body, leading in administration is a required duty and also a burden that pastors are called to bear.

Personal oversight is necessary for overseeing all layers and functions in ministry, i.e., worship, evangelism, teaching, mission, stewardship, and fellowship. A pastor's guiding love and guarded eyes keep watch to steer ministry ever closer to God's mission and vision for the church. The pastor not only leads to ensure smooth functioning of church operations, he also shepherds individual members in personal, intentional growth for discipleship (1Thes. 5:12-13, KJV). This represents pastoral duties that are in close alignment with functions of administration and membership management.

Pastoral Job Descriptions and Church Administration

There is always the "accountability to God" factor placed on the shoulders of pastors for members' growth. Pastors lead in teaching the tenants of gospel truth as well as in leading a generation of believers who likewise will exhort and teach others (2 Timothy 2:2, KJV).

Training in service, as clarified in Chapter Eight, is a vital component of pastoral leadership. Whether the pastor performs ongoing congregational training or serves to "oversee" the operational excellence of training of others (1 Timothy 5:17), he is responsible for administrative operations in leadership.

Leading the church to spiritual transformation is so vital to a church congregation that pastoral job announcements place a tremendous amount of weight in the job description on the responsibility to lead and administrate. Two examples of *Job Descriptions for a Pastor* are included in this chapter. Each displays the value churches are now placing on an incoming pastor's abilities to serve in the capacities of leadership and administration. The descriptions are useful guides to help a church in designing an announcement when the need arises.

The first Job Description listed can be Googled online.[71]

Example #1 - Pastoral Job Description for a Pastor

Special Note:
"Pastor", "Elder" and "Bishop" all refer to the same office. These terms are used interchangeably and often qualified/implied with the use of the word "overseer". Although the term pastor is commonly used today as the title of the spiritual overseer of a congregation, it was probably not intended in scripture to be a title but to be descriptive of what the office does.

Bylaws Description of Pastor
The Pastor is responsible for leading the church body in functioning as a New Testament Church (1Peter 5:2-4, 1 Timothy3:1-16; 2 Timothy 4:2). The pastor is responsible for providing spiritual instruction and strategic leadership to the members, staff and ministries of the church. The Pastor serves as the administrative officer and supervisor of church staff and the Administrative Business Council. The pastor is not responsible for doing all the work, but for seeing that it is completed and done properly and in order (I Corinthians 14:40, NLT).

Service Title: Pastor
Ministry Purpose: To proclaim the gospel of Jesus Christ, to teach the biblical revelation, to engage in pastoral care, provide administrative leadership in all areas of church life and function, supervise paid church staff and conduct the ordinances and functions of worship.

Serving Relationships:

The pastor serves under the guidance of the Holy Spirit and the church body. He directly receives counsel from the deacons who serve the congregation. The pastor serves as the leader of the Administrative Business Council.

Example #2 – Pastoral Job Description for Pastor

This second job description was designed, written and utilized by the pastor search committee, where I served as a team leader and writer of the description announcement for the search. The announcement was developed when our congregation was seeking a pastor to fill the pastoral pulpit vacancy at the New Saint Hurricane Missionary Baptist Church located in Pine Bluff, AR, in 2013. The announcement was innovative and was created to answer needs in accordance with church ministry operations in place at the time of the search.

The following format was utilized in the completion of the first phase of the pastoral search committee protocol.

Submit the initial candidate pastoral application package by mail to:
New Saint Hurricane Missionary Baptist Church[72]
c/o Pulpit Search Committee
3319 South Ohio Street
Pine Bluff, AR 71601

Position Overview:

New Saint Hurricane Missionary Baptist Church of Pine Bluff, Arkansas is seeking a full-time pastor called by God to serve as the spiritual leader of the congregation. The pastor is responsible to God and the church to proclaim the gospel of Jesus Christ, to teach the Bible, to provide Christian leadership in all areas of the church and to engage in pastoral care of the congregation. The pastor is also responsible for oversight of the overall leadership of day-to-day operations of the church, of services, membership and promoting the spiritual interest and growth of the church.

Major Qualifications

- Ordained Baptist Minister who has thorough knowledge of all Baptist doctrine and beliefs;
- The ability to provide Bible-based teaching;
- Accessibility and sensitivity to the needs of all demographics within the congregation;
- The ability to prepare and deliver biblically sound, inspirational, and Spirit-filled sermons;
- A vision for growing church membership that is rooted in the Word of God;
- The ability to identify and communicate assessed goals and effective strategies for leading the church through change;
- Strong commitment to providing ongoing discipleship training for ministry leaders including deacons, trustees and associate ministers;
- A commitment to increasing the numbers and spiritual development of youth and young adults in the congregation;
- A commitment to Christian education, missions, and evangelism;
- Exceptional standards of personal character, ethics and integrity;
- Demonstrates competence in leadership and management, communications (oral and written), interpersonal relations with the congregation and the secular community.
- Strong commitment to denominational affiliations including local district, state, and national relationships.

Minimum Qualifications

- Seminary trained, Masters of Divinity degree preferred
- Previous pastoral experience (or other Baptist church relevant leadership experience)
- Minimal of five years pastoral experience.

How to Apply

All interested and qualified persons must submit an initial candidate package consisting of copies of the following information:

1. A current resume that includes a summary of relevant ministry, professional, and educational experience.
2. Copies of ministerial license and ordination certificate.
3. Copies of degree(s).
4. Three recommendation letters (clergy (1), layperson (1), and personal (1)).
5. A New Saint Hurricane application requested via email at newsthurricane@cablelynx.com.
6. Additional information may be required before interviews take place.

Each pastoral job description listed is useful if a church needs them for future reference.

The Pastor as Lead Church Administrator

Some pastors are natural administrators with special talents to set quality vision for the church. They may equally have the ability to operate efficiently as leaders who can advance the execution of visionary operations. These pastors usually possess unique qualities to guide church movements in designing statements for core values, vision and mission statements, and with constructing them to connect with ministries in the church. Persons with such exceptional capabilities can serve as executive pastors, as senior pastors or the pastor. With their aptitude and skill set, along with their natural inclination to inspire managerial skills, they may be involved in handling and maintaining supervision for most, if not all, of the operations in the church. This includes designing, orchestrating and setting parameters for each ministry within the congregation.

This practice can flow into managing all monies, controlling budgets, payroll and, even cash flow. This level of hands-on tasking into church administration activities can be quite top-heavy and could become somewhat worrisome. Many pastors today are finding themselves deeply steeped in administrative tasks more often than not; unfortunately, it follows that they find less time than they would appreciate for their primary roles in setting vision, preaching, teaching and caring.

The literature is quite diverse as to identify specific individuals who may be called upon to serve in capacities to support the various areas of church administration for a congregation. The most logical person would be the pastor, resulting from the responsibilities given to pastors for the work of the kingdom. Since preaching and study in the Word is weightier for spiritual outcomes than task-oriented work, a pastor's oversight could be enlarged by developing high capacity leaders to also serve in administrative capacities, thus becoming support to those who will report functions and duties directly to the pastor.

A church administrator can be an associate minister in the congregation; someone who may also have administrative skills. Another candidate could be an administrator trained from schooling who has obtained further course work in church administration. Additionally, even an office administrator whose job it is to maintain a watchful eye and keen insight with the pastor on all things of an administrative nature could serve as a church administrator.

I believe the highest calling of leadership is to unlock potential in others. Success for ministry can be determined by how many persons the leader brings with him in advancing gifts and abilities. A thoughtful pastor desires to be a leader maker. This is an individual who equips others to also lead the work. Pastors cast the vision. They maintain a steady focus on the work of the mission and all component parts therein; they also celebrate with capable leaders who function to carry through, on their behalf, the massive work of the church. This is characteristic of transformational pastoral leadership

Administration, although vital to supporting the efficient work of the church to serve people more effectively, is not the final outcome of accomplishments for the church. Administrative goals, objectives and procedures should be written and clarified for all to obtain a greater understanding of their value; as it regards organization, the administration of church affairs is to glorify God.

❖

CHAPTER TEN

Administrative Planning for Transformation

Transformation for Church and Community

Christian maturity to help meet needs for others is an intended outcome of growth in the church. As a result of new and existing life challenging problems, transformational ministry is required to address needs both in the church while also serving surrounding vulnerable communities. Caring leaders offer members opportunity to create ways to share their faith through acts of service that ministers to multiple adverse situations around them.

Every approach to service should meet the call to develop new capacity to bridge church and community in hope and delivery. Transformational approaches to the traditional service model are required with the assurance that they communicate the message to seek Christ, to change lives and provide opportunities for people to live as over comers in Christ.

The mission to grow God's kingdom requires the church to maintain engagements with people who mirror a continuous pursuit for the love of Christ. Questions leaders ask include how satisfied are they with their church's impact on members, on the spiritual life of the church and with the church's influence in the community. These questions seek answers to identifying areas of measurement for congregational success in kingdom living. Churches experiencing lives transformed throughout the congregation will reflect members who attend worship to participate in healing hands deliverance throughout the community during the week.

Transformational churches make a difference for others. Regardless of membership size, demographic makeup, or even economic, social and educational status, transformed redeemed members desire participation in both in reach and outreach ministries of the church. Reaching others fosters connectedness to maintain engagements with home mission, state, national, and global missions. Is there passion for the needy, the less fortunate; those among you and even those you may not know or may never meet? Having a real sense of community is major to aiding persons living alone and to accessing the needs of seniors by mobilizing everyone to give and support.

Several years ago, LifeWay Research set out on an ambitious project to find answers to these and other questions of similar concern to church reality in the twenty-first century. For their research, they completed 7,000 telephone surveys, 250 on-site interviews with Protestant pastors, and surveyed more than 15,000 church members.

They gathered massive amounts of both quantitative (numbers) and qualitative (human experience) data that gave them a better understanding of how God was working in many congregations. They discovered and shared their findings in their book *Transformational Church*.[73] What these authors discovered was that in spite of their imperfections, many churches were having a transformational impact for their members. These transformational churches measured their success by a *new scorecard* in three areas of focus: the individual, the local church assembly, and the community.[74]

The continuous growth of a church body of believers is evident in the masterful ways it reaches everyone who desires to hear with needs and passions to advancing the greater good for all within its reach. Disciples with a heart for healthy relationships within and without the walls of the building communicate that the church will continue to thrive even during times of turbulence and disorder. This should be noted as effort to continuously transform the church for growth; spiritually, numerically, financially, and through relationships of love for family and community.

Transformational Church Administration

> For the church to remain under the Lordship of Christ,
> His crucifixion and resurrection, the crucial theme of the
> "church in mission" stands as the banner of representation
> that the church is in continued pursuit to seek Christ.

Developing a church for transformational administration is synonymous to preparing the church in the delivery of messaging and ministry of Jesus to the world. Transformational church pastors pivot their ministries to focus on how church functions to serve the mission of Christ in fulfilling the Gospel mandate to minister to the needs of others. The church begins by formulating new readiness to train members for skills in transformational leadership. This focus includes targeting and building church character with an emphasis on spiritual growth that celebrates the Lord by extending love and mercy toward others.

Lyrics from a familiar song echoes sentiments that "Time is filled with swift transition, Naught of earth unmoved can stand, Build your hopes on things eternal, Hold to God's unchanging hand."[75] Such is true of the inevitable truths for churches to embrace love of Christ and love for service from multiple contemporary platforms.

Traditionally, the church has served communities as beacons of guiding lights and God's symbol of hope for many people, especially persons living in challenging communities throughout America and around the globe. This can be especially true for cultures serving populations with a need to connect with communities to improve civic engagement and concerns in social justice. Numerous societal changes, historically high concentration of poverty in rural and urban areas and adverse economic and educational policies are credible reasons to present the Gospel through methods leading to lasting transformation.

Steady shifts in increased cultural globalization are present day determiners in how people live and conduct their lives. These shifts have fostered new attitudes affecting significant change in the work of the church. Worldview emphases on materialism greatly impact social attitudes for long held traditional values. Today, less familiar ways of existing seem to work their way into the operations and culture of the local church.

More than at any other time in history, America, and much of the world, is experiencing a plethora of changes in staggering proportions. The term megachange is used to indicate vast transitions in business, government, the schools and the church. Revolutionary change of huge magnitude is taking place at every level of operation in business, industry and in our individual lives. The impact is also noticeable in the church.

As these changes become solidly defined in the external culture, their influence also impacts how churches shape their relevance to present Christ to a lost world. With a determination to live the gospel mission for why Christ came to the world, the church embraces a new perspective for saving lives and sharing hope. This renewed service model for a new generation of believers can be described as *transformational administration in ministry.*

Investing in church software management systems, connecting membership to new structures of organization, and responding to the needs of surrounding struggling communities are necessary components to a vision for churches as they address new steps to transformational administration.

Transformational administration begins by placing core value on building missional leadership skills into the core mindset of the church's vision for evangelism and stewardship. The church designs the vision for a work that shares God's mission with members who will become catalysts for transformation within the community. Planning with disciples to serve the many mission needs of fragmented people's lives require necessary resources from church finances, organizations, funders, donors, and even community influencers.

Pastors, denominational boards, and religious community leaders are challenged to ensure that regardless of the situational constraints surrounding new design in transformational ministry, the church remains on message with sound doctrinal truths to teach only Christ to its members. Old limitations from former means of worship and discipleship must now shift to managing from a transformational process that meets human needs of healing much suffering people will experience in their daily lives.

God's Word and Church Growth[76]

Scriptures are added to strengthen the teaching and understanding for what God says about equipping the church to mature in the power of the Lord.

> Acts 2:47 - (ESV) Praising God and having favor with all the people. And the Lord added to their numbers day by day those who were being saved.

> Ephesians 4:11-12 – (ESV) And he gave the apostles, the prophets, the evangelists, the shepherds and teachers, to equip the saints for the work of ministry, for building up the body of Christ.

Matthew 16:18 – (ESV) And I tell you, you are Peter, and on this rock I will build my church, and the gates of hell shall not prevail against it.

John 12:32 - (ESV) And I, when I am lifted up from the earth, will draw all people to myself.

1 Corinthians 3:11 - (ESV) For no one can lay a foundation other than that which is laid, which is Jesus Christ.

Acts 9:31 - (ESV) So the church throughout all Judea and Galilee and Samaria had peace and was being built up. And walking in the fear of the Lord and in the comfort of the Holy Spirit, it multiplied.

Romans 12:2 - (ESV) Do not be conformed to this world, but be transformed by the renewal of your mind, that by testing you may discern what is the will of God, what is good and acceptable and perfect.

Acts 2:42 - (ESV) And they devoted themselves to the apostles' teaching and the fellowship, to the breaking of bread and the prayers.

Acts 20:20-31 - (ESV) How I did not shrink from declaring to you anything that was profitable, and teaching you in public and from house to house, testifying both to Jews and to Greeks of repentance toward God and of faith in our Lord Jesus Christ. And now, behold, I am going to Jerusalem, constrained by the Spirit, not knowing what will happen to me there, except that the Holy Spirit testifies to me in every city that imprisonment and afflictions await me. But I do not account my life of any value nor as precious to myself, if only I may finish my course and the ministry that I received from the Lord Jesus, to testify to the gospel of the grace of God.

2 Timothy 3:16-4:5 - (ESV) All scripture is breathed out by God and profitable for teaching, for reproof, for correction,

and for training in righteousness, that the man of God may be competent, equipped for every good work. I charge you in the presence of God and of Christ Jesus, who is to judge the living and the dead, and by his appearing and his kingdom: preach the word; be ready in season and out of season; reprove, rebuke, and exhort, with complete patience and teaching. For the time is coming when people will not endure sound teaching, but having itching ears they will accumulate for themselves teachers to suit their own passions.

Titus 1:5 – (ESV) This is why I left you in Crete, so that you might put what remained into order, and appoint elders in every town as I directed you.

1 Timothy 4:13 – (ESV) Until I come, devote yourself to the public reading of scripture, to exhortation, to teaching.

Envisioning Spiritual Transformation

Several scriptures come to mind to apply principles of *organizational transformational theory* for envisioning mission for transformational church administration. Churches are not corporations, secular organizations or institutions for business. Local church assemblies utilize and rely upon spiritual principals to fulfill their purposes and meeting goals. Church structural organization develops members who characterize the mind of Christ in the church and the world. The nature and purpose of the church transform people to act as collaborators in the kingdom for service to Christ as they are needed.

Observe below how scripture undergirds new vision for a transformational church. The texts support framing curriculum for study and implementation in transformational administrative ministry. Exposition to the texts supports how to align God's Word with incorporating new initiatives into visionary administrative models.

1. Romans 12:2 – "The Apostle Paul admonished believers to not "copy the behavior and customs of this world, but let God transform you into a new person by changing the way you think. Then you will

learn to know God's will for you, who is good and pleasing and perfect (NLT)."

The Christian gradually matures to a life of sacrifice and self denial. An outward spiritual transformation in character and conduct follows the surrender to yielding oneself to God. The inner "renewing of the mind" is the necessary foundation for outward behaviors. Such transformation of the heart and will molds a likeness matching personal conduct to the character of Christ.

It is a lifelong process to be transformed from habits of a former way of thinking to living in newness of intentional transformational reality that benefits others on a daily basis. This quality in character is powerful to management in service, worship, and giving with fellow members in the assembly. Because of the sacred and unique nature of the church, the world will not understand the life living by the examples of Christ to establish believers who *live in His image*.

2. Acts 2:42 – "And they devoted themselves to the apostles' teaching and fellowship, to the breaking of bread and the prayers (ESV)".

Every function for the church is unto the glory and honor of Christ. A daily devotion to the Apostles' teachings indicates that members of the Early Church possessed desire to live in the presence of the Lord. Instructions in righteousness paired with fellowship and worship was the church's longing to hear and to follow Christ. Surrender to His will led to obedience from study and prayer. The willingness to conform accordingly was preached for understanding, for instruction and for correction. These are the actions of a church growing in the knowledge to live the way of the Lord.

Learning together brings with it a common bond of friendship and fellowship for knowledge and participation with others of like minded interests. The hope in glory is shared. Love for doctrine is shared. Families partake in communal gatherings; in breaking bread and making merriment with one another as sisters and brothers in Christ. Likewise, they prayed for one another in obedience to the Father, the Son and the Holy Spirit.

3. Acts 9:31 - "The church then had peace throughout Judea, Galilee, and Samaria, and it became stronger as the believers lived in the fear

of the Lord. And with the encouragement of the Holy Spirit, it also grew in numbers (NLT)."

The text describes a time during the Early Church movement when persecution had ceased for a period and peace was available for the church to experience deliverance and growth. Christians took advantage of opportunities to preach the gospel and to form new churches in surrounding areas, primarily throughout Judea, Galilee and even in Samaria (Acts 11:19; Acts 9, KJV).

Teaching and preaching increased the numbers in the church and many were strengthened and built up in their hope (Romans 14:19; Romans 15:2; 1 Corinthians 8:1, KJV). Such actions brought about a new way of living; new joy for spiritual uplift and freshness in relationships.

By their actions, the people gave reverence to the Lord for all he had provided for them. Their gratefulness led them to devote themselves to obedience to his commandments. The people experienced joy and peace in the Holy Ghost; their numbers were multiplied (John 14:16-17; Romans 5:1-5, KJV). This joy and peace led to harmony working together to accomplish the mandates of the work from administration to management to service.

The church today will increase numerically, financially and in ministry obligations when the people hear and follow God's will. However, a greater measurement of growth in congregational performance is that members mature in Christ to living as faithful witnesses for him. A daily plea from pastors, leaders, as well as the membership, is that God's Spirit increase in the midst of all graces associated with church administration and growth. The goal of all church enrichment is the phenomenal development of people with hearts to love and obey God.

Features of a Renewed Church Vision

Historically, the church has served as the spiritual agent of change for a community. Today, more than ever, given the increase in poverty, violence and injustice in the world, the Christian church is called upon to embrace, engage, and advance its obligations as the representative agent of community transformation. The church continues to follow the teachings of Christ to fulfill the gospel imperative to make the world a better place for people to live in justice, peace and harmony. Such a huge task for the church! Questions to consider include "how does the church answer the call to new vision as it seeks to design fresh ministries for active loving kindness in a difficult world."

A renewed vision begins by incorporating principles of organization to current ministry contexts for a smooth transition in administrative operations. Decisions are based on their relatedness to concepts of time, events, structure, process management, needed resources and the impact they have on mission, purpose and the entire system. Specific goals are attained from the readiness of the system to accomplish new experiences in serving. Visionary effectiveness is achieved when goals and objectives are identified, pursued, met, and accomplished. The connection to maintain in focus is that organizational design is continually guided by biblical doctrine for all ministries.

As change occurs, church leaders who forecast for the future determine how each new change may impact congregational thought. Many will desire to maintain ministry as it currently exists. Change is not easy. The idea to administrate for Excellency in the delivery of services must be well thought out and planned for with deliberate intent. Presenting the gospel in the most effective and engaging methods possible is of major concern for church leaders. Pastors and leaders are conscious of factors relating to time on task and membership engagement during cycles of learning to the degree that participation and achievement occur in all segments of the new system.

In order for ministry to proceed with success, operational construction will experience directional variance at different points in the administration of the process. It is at these places that pastors and team leaders seek out best practice efforts to reinvest in different methodologies for continuous gains with new ministry goals and objectives.

Improvements in ministry operations are measured by weighing what happens in the church to what God's Word and the lead of the Holy Spirit say are necessary for the church to advance and grow. If reset is in order, conduct reevaluation of needs. Relevant variables to assess will include viewing management, systems of structure, curriculum, service, core values and the people to be served. These are essential elements to evaluating the church's response to vision in respect to accomplishments, effectiveness, accountability, and for transformation.

Key factors required of a visionary design for transformational church administration.[77]

- Prayer for God's Word to increase among the membership.
- Preaching and teaching the gospel message to increase spiritual growth and maturity.
- Modeling and training membership in transformational leadership skills.
- Work in small groups and teams.
- Equip members to accomplish the work of the ministry.
- Teach and train workers how to serve God by serving and caring for others.
- Teaching members to discover their spiritual gifts.
- Seek key visionary hope for in reach ministry and outreach community engagement.

Start the redesigned experiences by conducting performance analyses in the present church culture. This will include deciding on an identified process, developing leadership teams, observing variables, and listing outcomes. Progress evaluation and accountability factors are also included in the process.

- Revisit the church's present vision and mission statements.
- Evaluate current systems of management; sort for needs assessment, accountability, ministry planning, and quality control measurements.
- Keep in mind what to advance forward and what can be discontinued.
- Explore the church's value for older traditional methods. Determine which ones are beneficial and which ones or presently useless.
- Design the strategic leadership and decision making process.
- Build the structures of operation within all levels of the process.
- Choose persons willing to share their time for service to a transformational model for inclusive community service.
- Create awareness of the change for the entire church body of believers.
- Make decisions to incorporate change into the fabric of the existing church culture.

Making the decision to incorporate transformational change in the existing church order requires several strategies that will include the following:[78]

➢ Alert the Organization
➢ Communicate the Vision
➢ Create a Sense of Urgency

- ➤ Manage the Planning and Execution Process
- ➤ Set a Strategic Plan for Change
- ➤ Empower Others to Act on the Vision
- ➤ Consolidate Improvements
- ➤ Institutionalize Change

Selecting and implementing change for church transformation are some of the most challenging undertakings a church will face. If the change involves the entire church, believers are encouraged to assist in replacing traditional established ways to embrace newer more effective opportunities for ministry. The transformational process can be challenging. Some are somewhat intimidating. A few may be difficult to carry out. Transformation for a new hope in vision for the future is however, accomplished through leadership momentum and the urgency of the church to respond to a renewed call in service.

Leaders skilled with wisdom for the church and armed with appropriate instructions guided by the Holy Spirit, will walk systematically with the membership to develop best practice methods and designs for the church to maintain its mission of growing in the kingdom for members and for the community.

Planning the Visionary Process

Leading a church into spiritual strategic transformation involves designing and integrating vision and mission processes with people, with ideas and with traditions. When the church considers transforming older traditional methods to new contemporary innovations, several important factors must be considered. The coordination of ministry as the church currently knows it and ministry as leadership desires to move into must be communicated, discussed and defined for positive congregational engagement. The idea is not seek to satisfy everyone as to make people happy; but instead to discern best methods to embrace teaching and learning that closely resemble lives of the people involved. How people conduct business in today's changing culture is clearly important for leaders of congregations to consider.

Changes in technologies, organizations, businesses, people, beliefs and values determine how leaders construct transitional strategies to coordinate with ministry when addressing change within the present order of operation.

A review on the process of organizational transformation points to reasons organizations must change. There are four major concepts for leaders to know and analyze before moving into new vision within the church. The concepts basic to building models of transformation include: strategic vision, strategic leadership, organizational decision making, and organizational excellence.

1. *Strategic vision* "provides a corporate sense of being and gives the organization (church) opportunity to evaluate its current alignment with its enduring purpose. Vision transcends day-to-day issues. Vision empowers and encourages leaders and followers to implement change.[79] Vision outlines what a church desires to be in the future. Strategic vision is "what the organization hopes to become; it is the vision today for the church of tomorrow." Strategic vision provides overview of where the church wants to be in a specific time in the future.

   Strategic vision offers principles for details contained in later sections of the strategic plan. The strategic vision can be short or long term, depending on the type and duration of the project being proposed. Strategic vision gives ideas for the direction and activities in ministry development. Generally included in a document or statement for all members to see is a *great good faith effort* to announce that decisions are made in accordance with the church's theology and shared mission.

2. *Strategic leadership* for transformational change is a complex undertaking. Strategic leadership tells how to organize and manage the desired change. Strategic leaders are committed to analyzing and implementing new ways to understand their congregations. Integrating a strategic vision within the environment involves specific and systematic management of all variables and ministry operations considered for change. The nature and scope of the change process will vary; some change is small and incremental while others are huge and invasive.

   A successful strategic leader will determine the best roll out route to present a change order to the congregation. The smooth debut will introduce transitional change to positively impact an embrace of needed change. A pastor's management style should connect to the spirit and readiness of the people. Because the strategic environment is in a state of constant change, strategic leaders make wise decisions to determine best practice methods for introducing and launching new initiatives in the church. The wise strategic leader considers answers to questions such as "What manageable steps do members hope to see from a transformational model of change for the church?"

The ideas presented come from successful leaders who observe key roles to play and the most appropriate time to unveil new change models. They understand when to change course on steps or ideas as they follow the lead of the Holy Spirit. They figure out what changes are necessary. They determine which ones are desirable. These leaders discern how to manage for optimum results. Strategic leaders decide when change should be broad-based; where inclusion of the general congregation is best. They know that it is important to avoid sending wrong messages.

Strategic planners bring together theory, research and years of working with churches facing change as a means to offer leaders practical diagnostic models to help churches lead change in a spiritual and healthy way. They wisely communicate knowledge that *best practice procedures* help people realize when an organization must change.[80]

3. *Organizational decision making* is the heart of all major processes within a framework of transformational change. If strategic visionary leadership is the head, surely, organizational decision making skills comprise the heart of the operation. All systems included within the design and lasting results of their impact in the church will be measured by the methodologies and administrative factors of the process. Decision making is huge business. It can be both complex and comprehensive at the same time. However, *if the transition to transform is embedded within an effective systems approach for management, there will be organizational success.* The key is in the process called *transition*. Transition moves operations from one space to another; from one level to the next; from one idea to the next new thought.

An organizational decision making process consists of design, methodology, approach, analysis, evaluation and follow up. Strong organizational change occurs when the systems of critical operation are managed effectively. Setting systemic reinforcements to the groundwork early in the process is basic to structuring understanding for management. Systemic reinforcements provide new proposals in knowledge to handle possible negative outcomes from variances in outcomes of implemented results.

Decision making is critical for leaders when deciding which contemporary innovations a church should wisely choose for the next stage in the process. Organizational decision making is essential to coordinating ministries across the church with one another. Cross teaching, cross training and mentoring for service are examples where strategic leadership team members accomplish more through collaboration and partnerships within their groups and throughout the congregation.

4. *Organizational Excellence* involves transforming the church by managing and coordinating all essential systems' variables for the maximum degree of success. *In Management Essentials for Church Ministries,* authors Michael J. Anthony and James Estep, Jr. [81] outlined and described operational design that successfully combined the laws of order to effective management for church transformation, both spiritually and operationally.

The work detailed principles of a systems approach in organizational management for the church. The structure began with an administrative model that operates from four basic elements: *Scripture, Ideas, Things, and People.* Each element is vital to setting up the big picture of an organization for the success of the whole. Without either of the four, that is, leaving one out, the entire organization is placed in jeopardy of being incomplete in both scope and content.

All elements of church operation are required to provide adequate decision making from leaders and team members as they participate in the process of change. Each component part in the organizational design coordinates to produce administrative functioning for management equilibrium. Balance of all measured and thought out parts bring stability to the organization.

To cast such a broad, yet comprehensive net to setting the house in order from a program of systems management requires diligent labor and commitment. Organizational excellence proposes that church leaders pair principles of organizational design with theological foundations as the necessary underpinning of biblical reinforcement.

A concluding reflection is that symmetry in design to carry out God's good plans for church transformation is second only to the successful communication of the messaging to teach people to know and love Christ. The church must always remember why a choice to design a framework in transformational ministry was important in the first place.

Writing Mission and Vision Statements

What is the difference between vision and mission? A church's mission statement declares what direction the leadership desires to go in vision and clarifies if the vision is in line with God's purposes for their lives. Organizations utilize vision and mission statements to set order to their goals, objectives, and their long range planning.

What the Bible Says about Vision[82]

Proverbs 29:18 - (ESV) Where there is no prophetic vision the people cast off restraint, but blessed is he who keeps the law.

Luke 4:18-19 - (ESV) The Spirit of the Lord is upon Me, because He has anointed Me to proclaim good news to the poor. He has sent Me to proclaim liberty to the captives and recovering of sight to the blind, to set at liberty those who are oppressed, to proclaim the year of the Lord's favor.

Psalm 91:1-16 - (ESV) He who dwells in the shelter of the Most High will abide in the shadow of the Almighty. I will say to the LORD, "My refuge and my fortress, my God, in whom I trust." For He will deliver you from the snare of the fowler and from the deadly pestilence. He will cover you with His pinions, and under His wings you will find refuge; His faithfulness is a shield and buckler. You will not fear the terror of the night, nor the arrow that flies by day.

Revelation 14:12 – (ESV) Here is a call for the endurance of the saints, those who keep the commandments of God and their faith in Jesus.

Colossians 3:17 – (ESV) And whatever you do, in word or deed, do everything in the name of the Lord Jesus, giving thanks to God the Father through Him.

Genesis 1:26 – (ESV) Then God said, "Let us make man in our image, after our likeness. And let them have dominion over the fish of the sea and over the birds of the heavens and over the livestock and over all the earth and over every creeping thing that creeps on the earth.

1 Corinthians 1:17 – (ESV) For Christ did not send me to baptize but to preach the gospel, and not with words of eloquent wisdom, lest the cross of Christ be emptied of its power.

Habakkuk 2:2-3 – (ESV) And the Lord answered me: "Write the vision; make it plain on tablets, so he may run who reads it. For still the vision awaits its appointed time; it hastens to the end—it will not lie. If it seems slow, wait for it; it will surely come; it will not delay.

The Power of Vision

Vision outlines what a church desires to become in the future. Vision takes into consideration long range goals and short term objectives to be obtained and mastered. Vision is a clear, challenging picture of the future of the ministry and what is perceived that it will be. Vision asks of us to answer the question "what kind of church would we like to be?" Vision changes over time and must be renewed, adapted, and adjusted to the cultural context in which the church conducts business.

In his chapter, *"Developing a Vision: What Kind of Church Would We Like to Be?* from his book, Advanced Strategic Planning,*[83]* Aubrey Malphurs declares that vision is essential to the future of a church. Unlike qualities for values, mission, and purpose, vision is more often subject to change. It is dynamic and active as opposed to being fixed and unchanging.

Over time, the vision must be renewed, adapted, and adjusted to the cultural context in which the congregation lives and worships. These changes take place only at the margins of the vision, not at its core, which is the church's mission. The core, for example, the Great Commission, will not change. Vision provides a picture of what mission will look like as it is realized in the lives of the people in the church and the surrounding community.

The Importance of Vision

Vision is of utmost importance to leaders and their ministry. *"The most important factor in vision is to move the organization toward greatness. A vision that directs an organization toward mediocrity is difficult and does not gain enthusiasm among the team."* [84] A vision statement tells what the organization wants to become and how it wants to be viewed. To be effective, vision must be optimistic and forward thinking, yet it is realistic and reachable. An unrealistic vision statement has no value for anyone. A vision for the church should be aggressive, yet attainable. A church will never be greater than its understood vision.

The Effective Mission Statement

What is an effective mission statement? While the vision sets the target goal, mission statements guide year-to-year operations. Mission statements involve reaching achievable goals in the church. Accomplishing church Mission requires that leadership engage people, strategies, staff, office administrative work, and other identifiable logistics necessary to accomplishing the grand goals of the organization. Mission is a broad, brief, biblical statement of what the church is supposed to be doing. Mission focuses on the functional questions, "Who are we?" "What are we suppose to be doing?"

Mission is present day to day focus and describes how a church plans on achieving what is visualized through vision. Persons with common interests in the success of the church are directly interested in mission statements because they can clearly articulate what the church is doing, how it is going to go about doing it, and ultimately why it is purposefully engaged in getting the work done .

Key questions to answer in a mission statement include: (1) What is the purpose and role of the local church? (2) Who does the church seek to serve? and (3) What benefits will the church provide for the people who attend? Mission statements answer present concerns about where the church is at any given time, what is being done about the needs and why is the church is engaged or not engaged with a problem or need at any given time.

The primary difference between a vision and mission statement is the timeline. In general, a mission statement defines what an organization is currently doing, while a vision statement is basically the ultimate goal of what they would like to accomplish. The mission statement tells what people do to achieve the vision.

SECTION FOUR

A Transformational Model for Management

❖

CHAPTER ELEVEN

Transforming Organizational Structures

Structure is the method churches use to organize activities to pursue purpose. Structure provides efficiency in maximizing opportunity to further God's ordained mission. It is the roadmap of descriptive markers to identify component parts of all that is *at the heart of the church's intent to reach, teach and transform persons in the way Christ intended.* The church has a mandate to <u>only</u> accomplish its <u>one</u> purpose. Organization relates to how the church pursues that purpose with the aid of the Holy Spirit and empowered quality leadership. Organizational management brings clarity to the process serious minded leaders need to master concerns with *messaging, continuity and follow-up.*

Principles of Organizational Structure

Study in human and organizational development helps church leaders prepare mentally and spiritually for work in the kingdom. It is here that they gain insight imperative to identify how both organizational design and systems management are interrelated in the pursuit to structure God's purposeful work in the church.

Application from this knowledge relates principles of systems in the church to accomplishments of Christ on behalf of the church body. His birth, His ministry, His death, burial, resurrection, and His ascension to heaven is God's intended message for the church. Knowing the relatedness of both structure and purpose leads to the application of principles and merits for organizational theory to explain how they are embedded into a design for purposeful ministry organization.

Studies in principles of organizational systems management help church leaders prepare for long-term process planning. Grounded in models that influence policy for solutions, organizational theory is important to affect issues important to accomplishing spiritual vision and to thusly relate them to principles of church organizational structure. The people they serve, the linkages in the delivery of content, spiritual growth and membership participation are valuable elements leaders consider when redesigning management in the church.

Organizational structural changes have advanced from earlier stiff, hierarchical systems commonly found in the industrial age to more flexible and inclusive systems existing in today's technological modern age.[85] These changes over time have had profound impact on how organizations conduct business including how the church body of believers relate to systems of operation for ministry leadership and development within the congregation and surrounding communities.

Theories in Organizational Development

Prior to a discussion of church organizational structure and its systematic movements in ministry expansion, a review of historically applied theories in human and organizational development will reinforce understanding of the process. Applying organizational development to ministry, in theory, adds value to biblical perspectives when engaging in spiritual principles and mandates significant to setting the Lord's house in order for kingdom service.

Organizational theory is the *study of the development of all systems of interrelated parts functioning* within organizations. There are four major theories that contribute to an understanding of organizations and their structure. These theories are classical theory, human relations theory or what was called neo-classical theory, decision making theory, and modern systems theory.

Over time, significant changes in systems of management have become useful to providing insight into critical issues of organizational research and theoretical design. Contemporary predictors for organizational effectiveness serve transformational leaders with new paradigms of thought that encourages cultures to seek contemporary innovative energy for strategic organizational change.

Major features of organizational composition and their relationship to final outcomes help leaders plan for future accomplishments in organizational effectiveness. This knowledge influences primary and secondary outcomes within the congregation as well as with stakeholders connected to the life of the church.

Systems can be highly bureaucratic and top heavy (pastor and appointed leadership) in terms of who decides what will occur or they can be dynamic and transformational (pastor, leadership teams, membership inclusion and even community) in application for a variety of decision making opportunities.

Classical Organization Theory

Developed during the first half of the twentieth century, Classical Organization Theory gave business, industry, education, and even the church grand models of management from what was termed as scientific management, bureaucratic theory and administrative theory. *Scientific management theory* sought to pair the best people for the right job or task. Production was important. *Bureaucratic theory* involved establishing a hierarchy to describe the division of labor and recognized the importance of specialization. *Administrative theory* established a rather strict set of management principles that applied to all organizations.

Neoclassical Organization Theory

Improvements in organization theory led to a new focus. The renewed energy was now on what was occurring within the work *environment*. Productivity improves in an atmosphere where unity and consistency operates in combination with known organizational values for meaning when purpose is on ready display. According to Neoclassical Organization Theory, the organization is the social system and its performance is affected by varying degrees in *human actions*.

Organizations succeed within a cohesive environment where followers are accepting of leadership authority. Key principles toward the success include: (1) emphasizing differences between people to create factors of distinctiveness as effective motivators; and (2) resolving conflict to help develop new ideas that build stronger working alliances. Another principle key to the theory is the emphasis on social interactions, participative management and decision-making.

The principle key to this theory is maintaining balance, stability, and peace within the organization. There is a sense of steadiness for the organization when group members consider others in similar relatable ways as they think of themselves.

"For by the grace given to me I say to everyone among you not to think of himself more highly than he ought to think, but to think with sober judgment, each according to the measure of faith that God has assigned"(Romans 12:3, ESV) is an excellent example of scripture relating to principles of Neo Classical Organizational Theory.

Contingency/Decision-Making Theory

Followers of contingency theory, also referred to as the decision-making theory, view conflict as something that requires continuous layers of management. This theory espouses the principle that organizations act rationally to adapt to impending environmental changes. From this theory, effectiveness in the organization is generally determined by the strength of the leader.

The basis of contingency theory is that there is no one best way to handle any task or process. It recognizes that the future and therefore *change*, is imminent. Movement for this theory notes that regardless to how effective or even efficiently a process has been planned, the future and the ultimate unknown, may arrive with the need to devise new methods in design and operation.

Contingency, by the very nature of its definition, alerts the organization to the possibility to *be on the alert*. Organizers should be on the lookout for unforeseen emergencies looming over the horizon; waiting for variances to occur. Whether organizing an entire church planting project or planning a new ministry work flow, the best solutions could easily be influenced by internal or external inconsistencies. When compromises occur, prior predetermined methods and even leadership management style may risk losing their presumed effectiveness. Pastors and leaders therefore will need to consider adjusting their managerial methods and techniques based on the conditions of constraints around them.

Fred Fiedler is a theorist whose Contingency Trait Theory was the precursor to his Contingency Management Theory. Fiedler also believed that a direct correlation exists between a leader's personality and the leader's effectiveness to influence the work of the organization.[86] Here again, leadership adaptability paired with expert skills as quality influencers for the greater good are very important.

Modern Systems Theory

Foundation to the Modern Systems Theory is the principle that all component parts of an organization are interrelated, one with another Modern Systems Theory was developed in the early 1960s.[87] Modern Systems Theory operates from both a conceptual and an analytical framework of *relatable variables.* These variables pinpoint both meaning and identifiable purposes that integrates all parts to the whole in structural design. Modern Systems Theory defines the organization by connecting each equally manageable part to the operation of the complex whole. This purpose is to maintain logical order for sequence in structure. The system is open to interacting with surrounding environments to sustain itself for growth. Assembling or combining all parts in the organization forms the system's framework for the entire operation.

The different parts of the system (the church) are called sub-systems (the ministries, administration, management, teams, leadership). These sub-systems are all interrelated to function for the good of the whole (the mission, the edification and building up of the body of Christ). Additionally, all sub-systems (the ministries and the design models of administration and management) are arranged according to a scheme (their function and task in relationship to organizational structure for the whole) so that the complete system (the body of Christ existing as the church) is more than just a sum of its visible parts.

As the Spirit of the Living Lord leads in teaching, preaching and mentoring, the church grows and matures in spiritual readiness to function for kingdom growth. As its individualized parts (the people) change and grow in maturity to follow Christ, so will the power and works become manifest for all to see and believe.

From this perspective, preaching and teaching of theology for the application of all embedded works in the delivery of the kingdom of God, the Modern Systems Theory operates to ensure efficient functioning of the church "until we all reach unity in the faith and in the knowledge of the Son of God," (Ephesians 4:13, NIV) as a complex whole.

God's Word and Organizational Theory[88]

Habakkuk 2:2 - (ESV) And the LORD answered me: "Write the vision; make it plain on tablets, so he may run who reads it.

Proverbs 13:4 – (ESV) The soul of the sluggard craves and gets nothing, while the soul of the diligent is richly supplied.

Proverbs 6:6-11 – (ESV) Go to the ant, O sluggard; consider her ways, and be wise. Without having any chief, officer, or ruler, she prepares her bread in summer and gathers her food in harvest. How long will you lie there, O sluggard? When will you arise from your sleep? A little sleep, a little slumber, a little folding of the hands to rest.

1 Corinthians 15:58 – (ESV) Therefore, my beloved brothers, be steadfast, immovable, always abounding in the work of the Lord, knowing that in the Lord your labor is not in vain.

Matthew 24:44-51 – (ESV) Therefore you also must be ready, for the Son of Man is coming at an hour you do not expect. "Who then is the faithful and wise servant, whom his master has set over his household, to give them their food at the proper time? Blessed is that servant whom his master will find so doing when he comes. Truly, I say to you, he will set him over all his possessions. But if that wicked servant says to himself, 'My master is delayed.'

Exodus 18:13-27 – (ESV) The next day Moses sat to judge the people, and the people stood around Moses from morning till evening. When Moses' father-in-law saw all that he was doing for the people, he said, "What is this that you are doing for the people? Why do you sit alone, and all the people stand around you from morning till evening?" And Moses said to his father-in-law, "Because the people come to me to inquire of God; when they have a dispute, they come to me and I decide between one person and another, and I make them know the statutes of God and his laws." Moses' father-in-law said to him, "What you are doing is not good."

Romans 12:11 – (ESV) Do not be slothful in zeal, be fervent in spirit, serve the Lord.

Genesis 1:1-5 – (ESV) In the beginning, God created the heavens and the earth. The earth was without form and void, and darkness was over the face of the deep. And the Spirit of God was hovering over the face of the waters. And God said, "Let there be light," and there was light. And God saw that the light was good. And God separated the light from the darkness. God called the light Day, and the darkness he called Night. And there was evening and there was morning, the first day.

Luke 14:28 – (ESV) For which of you, desiring to build a tower, does not first sit down and count the cost, whether he has enough to complete it?

2 Timothy 1:7 – (ESV) For God gave us a spirit not of fear but of power and love and self-control.

1 Corinthians 14:40 – (ESV) But all things should be done decently and in order.

Applying Organizational Theory to Church Structure

It has been my desire from the beginning of this writing to communicate the necessity to intentionally combine God's mission from biblical theology with practical principles of transformational leadership. The combination of the two frames of identification presents application for excellence in church administration and management. *HONOR to the Great Head of the Church* is an insistence that order, sequence, operation and achievements are accomplished when the church functions from a kingdom mindset to serve God's people in this present age.

This section of Chapter Eleven presents an integration of systems from organizational theory as they are incorporated to form a theoretical framework for the operation of church in management. Highlighted from three theories of human and organizational development, insight into the relationships between theory, scripture and basic designs of church structure are presented to combine proper administration to management for ministry outcomes.

The task is to now pair historical theories of human thought with kingdom principles in doctrine that will directly impact messaging and daily operations in the church.

This principle will show the connectedness between organizational theories in management to God's messaging of His mission from theological doctrine. The purpose is to now superimpose a theological foundation to explanations of organizational theory presented previously in this chapter. The overlay is necessary to further describe the application of scientific structures and their relationship to transformational leadership management for the church.

In Chapter Nine, The Church and Administration, ministries were identified and paired with scripture and organizational realities to list how the church, from its inception, was aligned with systems of organization to accomplish the work of mission and doctrine on behalf of Christ. *Four categories of vocabulary associated with leadership, administration and systems management were created and listed to indicate how scripture pairs with vision for organizational reality within the church.*

The categories were viewed in terms of their relatedness to each other and to theoretical systems of ministry organization. The four categories of vocabulary listed and the headings for their placements were:

- Leadership and Management- *Leadership, Vision, Organizational Systems, Strategies*
- Leadership, Administration, and Management - *Management, Service Models, Decision Making, Building Teams, Procedures*
- Administration, and Management - *Ministry, Teaching, Training, Mentoring*
- Leadership, Administration, and Management - *Priorities on People, Members Responsibilities, Staff Appointments*

These four vocabulary categories will now be further delineated to correlate their existence within the three distinct areas of human and organizational development, three major components of church ministry operations. The organizational development content areas are (1) human development, (2) spiritual development, and (3) organizational development.

A careful study in applied theories in human and organizational development will view closely the merits of systems management to the teaching of Christ, to salvation and maturation in doctrine and to the creative alliance of their relatedness to masterful organization. The value applied here is to acknowledge their impact on leadership interpretation and decision making for ministry.

In a paper presented during my PhD. study in Ministry Leadership, I wrote to address how theories in organization and human development correlate with scripture to move members into disciplines for maturation in spiritual formation. The tie-in of both behaviors evolves to help individuals live a life developed in discipleship and spiritual transformation.[89]

Content areas for human development, organizational development, and spiritual development were analyzed to detail how these theories function as integrated spaces into all systems of the church, including those relating to spiritual growth and development. Summary findings from the paper are presented here to support clarity for how the dynamics of human organizational theory and behavioral management can significantly affect the life and health of a congregation.[90]

I. *Human Development - The Theory*

This field of study defines theories, perspectives, and principles associated with human life-span development from the time of conception to the end of life (Papalia, Olds, & Feldman).[91] Theory is described here as a means to place emphasis on expanding thought relative to human development for infants, children, adolescences, as well as a new focus in emerging adulthood, and adult development. Cultural influences were included in the research to share how lifestyle shapes interpretation of though and perspectives.

Areas relatively new to the study of human development is study in Developmental Behavioral Neuroscience (DBN), which is synonymous with human development issues found in biology, psychological, social-cultural development, social interaction, and in the evolution of social systems. Issues associated with DBN include developmental disorders, particular disorders of language, learning, perception, and social behavior. Aging, social attachment, temperament and personality are also included to shape thought for theories relating to normal and when necessary, disordered development associated in these constructs.

The need to identify these newer areas in human development is important to understanding advanced offerings of evolutionary care found in today's disciplines of human psychological need.

Human Development – Its Impact for the Church

Individual behavior, which is the foundation of all organizational performance and the understanding of the physiological and psychological systems of behavior are crucial to effective church management. The church is built entirely on the behaviors of what happened at Calvary and the resurrection; however, a study of human behavior is crucial to management concerns in ministry organizations. Individual behavior is closely tied to an understanding of personality factors leading to positive or negative influences affecting growth and maturity of members in the church.

Because the spiritual health of the church depends in large part on people performance, pastors and church leaders need more than a passing knowledge of the issues effecting what happens from the actions of individual members. It is vitally important that pastors possess understanding of how personality and attitudes affect individual behaviors within the congregation.

There are five sources of personality development found in the field of human development: *heredity, environment, family, group memberships, and life experiences.* These sources affect many facets of conduct from church members throughout the congregation. Secondary factors such as outcomes derived from trust or mistrust, competency, courage, self-control, integrity, fidelity, despair and productivity are included in leadership discussions for how members grow and influence conditions which affect the overall health and spiritual vitality of the church.

II. Spiritual Development – The Theory

Spiritual development as a component to theory relating to human and organizational development has been discussed fairly comprehensively in the works of Kenneth O. Gangel and James C. Wilhoit.[92] Growth in spiritual development is the basis for all biblical study necessary to transform believers to become individuals who witness to the world for Christ with their words and their lives.

These authors offer believers hope in establishing personal spiritual maturity as an alternative to *humanistic education; a secular view of religion* that can essentially rob churches of their *power to effect change.* The editors established in their writings, fundamental truths about basic aspects of spiritual formation. They give insight into the definition, history, theology, worship, spiritual disciplines and stages of development for maturing spiritually. Spiritual development systematically provides understanding of God's grace for the transformation of man. In doing so, learners are given significant ideas to aid in moving forward as believers.

Spiritual development answers concerns when people are seeking truths to navigate issues of life such as: "We do not have the answers, we do not know what will make things better, but we are assured that God knows. We serve in confidence that He cares and He works things out on our behalf. Our trust is in Him; try as we might, we fall short. We therefore live for Him, in Him and because of Him."

Another factor relating to spiritual formation is meditating in His love in acts of corporate and personal worship. Meditation is a connecting link between prayer and Bible study. Meditation expresses the idea that prayer and study are linked together by time spent with the Savior. Careful thought about what we read and what we ask of God renews us throughout the day and gives peace for all that we seek.

Gangel and Wilhoit[93] conclude that "it is OK to ask God for things we need and desire." They supplied opinions backed with scripture to teach differences between praise and petition factors. The authors added that generally mature Christians perceive that praise to God is on a higher order than mere petition to God. But truth bears out that going to God in confidence, knowing that He hears when we express our needs to Him, gives us assurance that as we ask in Jesus' name, we also receive (John 14:13-14, John 16:24, 1 John 5:14) .

Spiritual Development – Its Impact for the Church

Spiritual development occurs when individuals make a decision to become spiritual seekers. The church believes that as it engages members in the pursuit of Bible knowledge, members are filled with the indwelling spirit of God's holiness. As knowledge is paired with love for God, hope in the resurrection, obedience to the message of the cross and to submission to His will results in spiritual development throughout the church body. Teaching and training in disciplines of formation, spiritual growth and development is revealed in the hearts and the actions of member believers.

Spiritual development is proof of the authority and power of the Holy Spirit is at work in the church. It is recognition to leaders that transformation in Christ from within the membership is taking place. Spiritual development advances all basic rules to share truths needed for excellence in communication, devotion and fellowship. Launching new endeavors, mission advancements and worship, teaching and service from the central core of spiritual growth are vastly impactful to effective ministry.

III. Organizational Development (OD) – The Theory

Solidly recognized as a distinct field of study, the subject of organizational development (OD) is described as the systematic process of improving organizations through carefully planned and implemented methods which seek to advance profitability, productivity, team effectiveness, morale and quality of work. In their resource, Practicing Organization Development: A Guide for Consultants, authors Rothwell, Sullivan & McLean shared methods and strategies of implementation used by organizations to produce the much desired change process. [94]

With a focus always on the words "systematic, planned process, or effort," Organizational Development targets outcomes to implement strategies today that will find value for adequacy in the future. Planners who seek to manage Organizational Development operations possess knowledge of the plan, know how it works and are equipped with a skill set to implement it for all constituents to be served. They may have skills in the workings of the organization's current state of affairs or be willing to obtain such needed training. Solid Organizational Development principles and recommended solutions to achieve new and updated visionary outcomes are excellent methods to achieve common sense results for needed changes as they exist in the environment.

Organizational Development – Its Impact for the Church

Questions leaders ask here is "what will we do to present a plan that people will participate in and follow?" Will God get the glory from our labor? By its very nature, change equals resistance. Pastors serve as lead change agents who will steer the ship and navigate stubborn and even unwilling waters of resistance. Answers come when pastors, church consultants, leaders and members work out solutions to diagnose and deal with each resisting factor as they arise in the process. Prayer without ceasing is the first and final call to action.

Several marketing tools are available to help churches recognize human development, spiritual and operational factors that push against or serve as opposition to change. Helping the church move into *transformational ways of thinking* fosters the use of advanced approaches to organizational management.

Organizational Structures for Your Church

Selecting and designing the appropriate organizational outcomes systems of management will be a final stage necessity in the coordination to align for ministry objectives. Church organizational flow charts can provide excellent models to show descriptors indicating *who does what, who they report to, and what is the nature and extent of their responsibilities.* Scheduling the anticipated outcomes is equally as valuable to obtaining desired results as planning and designing for them with leaders and supporting team members.

Transforming old traditional organizational systems of management to newer organizational models for ministry acknowledges the desires of churches today to more fully bring their work in alignment with scripture. Mirroring ministry to the context of scripture for spiritual growth indicates that special attention has been given to grow members to adapt to functions that reflect the mission of God. Key vocabulary terms relating church activity to biblical mandates are essential to building new systems that seek to keep the church focused on meaning and messaging.

Throughout each chapter of this volume, defining critical church ministry functions has been communicated as being valuable to always live for Christ in the midst of daily operations for the church. Incorporating terminology that relates to the hope of spiritual living is timeless in scope and functionality. They will never lose value regardless of ongoing world traditions. These terms have been identified to maintain godly messaging connecting church structure in ministry to what God says.

A brief list of vocabulary useful to identify areas of organization for a new focus in organizational design and structure is included below. Choose from these and other biblically functioning words to address a future outline in organizational design for advancing new ministries in your congregation when the need arises.

Vocabulary that Highlights Biblical Functions Rather than Traditional Hierarchy

- Evangelism – The spreading of the gospel of Jesus Christ.
- Preaching - To advocate with urgency to believe and receive the gospel of Jesus Christ.
- Worship – To express reverence and adoration in public and in private devotion.
- Prayer – A solemn plea to request desires, hopes and to express commitment.
- Teaching the Bible – Systematically educating others in the Word of God.
- Repentance – Expressing regress, sorrow and remorse for sin. Atonement.
- Confession - A public and personal declaration to acknowledge Jesus as Lord.
- Service - Functions to help, wait on, carry out, assist, and aid in ministry.
- Spiritual Growth – To increase in the knowledge of our Lord Jesus. To develop in grace. To learn how to live for Christ. To glorify Him with our lives.
- Giving – Being generous in our bounty unto the Lord for the sake of the kingdom.
- Discipleship - A life transformed to living for Christ and following Christ.
- Fellowship – Meeting together and sharing the same values with other followers of Jesus Christ.
- Servant Leadership – The idea that the primary goal (obligation) of the leader is to serve. Serving others as a direct way of following Christ; who came not to be served but to indeed serve.
- Planning – Systematic process to organize with details. The methods to make plans.
- Evaluating – Using a standard to determine, assess, or formulate a worth or value.
- Team Building – Strengthen people to work together effectively for a common goal.

- Discipline – Conduct conducive to obeying rules and following systems of behavior.
- Community - Sense of fellowship with others living in close proximity to one another; persons sharing much in common with one another.

The terms listed here carry significant correlations to the eternal purpose and design of the church. They are essential for church organizations to communicate the message of accountability within the ministry for spiritual growth. They are useful to keep focus on the deliverance of mission in the church. Greater insight for tasks in ministry supports present and future need to transform from a traditional structural model to one that focuses on what the church means regardless of the times presented.

> This new emphasis on ministry function for purpose is transforming! Its revelation is revolutionary! It is absolutely significant to building structure, incorporating management, and designing follow-up with accountability from a place that teaches our Lord Jesus. Designing organizational structure in the church that centers on biblically spiritual functions of the church is major to moving the local assembly, throughout the ages, closer to its missional purpose and ordained destiny.

Two Organizational Flow Charts from the New St. Hurricane Missionary Baptist Church of Pine Bluff, AR are included to present two service models that served the organizations of the church.[95] The first model presents a traditional organizational chart to indicate auxiliary management from a fundamental traditional perspective. It was productive and served well in alignment with earlier vision and mission plans of the church. However, when a newer service leadership mission was incorporated into the character and culture for the church, a biblically functioning focused model was designed to place stronger emphasis on transformational service to Christ and purpose for serving others in the kingdom.

Look for similarities as well as differences found from the two models for the same congregation.

2017 New St. Hurricane Leadership Teams © 2017

Pastor

Director of Ministries

Pastoral Ministries	Brotherhood Ministry	Church Service Ministries	Christian Education Ministries	Worship Ministries	Outreach Service Ministries
• Associate Ministers	• Men's Ministry	• Service Coordination Ministries	• Sunday School	• Media Ministry	• Boy Scouts
• Church Office Administrator	• Young Men's Ministry	New Members Ministry	• Vacation Bible School	• Drama Ministry	• Girl Scouts
• Deacon Ministry		Keep in Touch Ministry	• Women Ministry	• Praise Dance Ministry	
• Trustee Ministry		Couples Ministries	Women Missionary Society	• Praise Team Ministry	
• Church Mother's Ministry		Singles Ministries	Women Mentoring	• Inspirational Choir	
• Baptismal Ministry		College Students Ministry	• Children and Youth Ministry	• Men's Choir	
		W.O.R.D. Fitness Ministry	HYPE Teens	• Youth Choir	
		Nurses Ministry	HYPE Middlers		
		Nursery Ministry	HYPE Elementary		
		• Service Helps Ministries			
		Ushers Ministry			
		Hospitality Ministry			
		Culinary Ministry			
		Decoration Ministry			
		Transportation Ministry			
		Parking and Security Ministries			

New St. Hurricane MBC - A traditional organizational chart to highlight a ministry management model derived from Classical Organizational Theory. Note the relatedness to a management hierarchy perspective. Organizational church models to design ministry along this order served congregations well beginning around the Industrial Age and on to the Modern Management Age. Developed during the first half of the 20th Century, Classical Organization Theory gave business, industry, education and even the church grand models of management from what was termed as scientific management, bureaucratic theory and administrative theory.

New St. Hurricane MBC Traditional Organizational Model

A Traditional Organizational Chart to Highlight Ministry Management Model from Classical Organizational Theory. Note the Relatedness to a Management Hierarchy Perspective. Pine Bluff, AR. [96]

2020 New St. Hurricane Leadership Teams

Pastor

In Coordination with Church Leadership Team

Operations	Family Ministries	Church Service Ministries	Christian Education/Discipleship	Worship Arts Ministries	Outreach/Evangelism Ministries
Administrative Assistant	HYPE NURSERY	Service Coordination Ministries	Christian Life School	Media Ministry	Boy Scouts
Finace Admin	HYPE Elementary	Deacons Ministry	Sunday School	Drama Ministry	Girl Scouts
Trustees	HYPE Middle School	Baptismal Minstry	Vacation Bible School	Pantomine Dance Ministry	550 Fifth Sundays Outreach
Facilities Management	HYPE High School	New Members Ministry		Praise Team Ministry	Greeters Ministry
Maintenance	Marriage	Keep in Touch Ministry	Life Groups	Inspirational Choir	Welcome Minitry
Custodial	Young Adults	Singles Ministry	Women	Men's Choir	Visitor Follow up
New/Existing Facilities	Family Conference	College Students Ministry	Men	Youth Choir	
Leadership Team		W.O.R.D. Fitness Ministry	Young Adults		HYPE Center
		Nurses Ministry			Afterschool
			HYPE Night for Students		Coding Ministry
		Service Helps Ministries	Teens		Athletics
		Ushers Ministry	Middle School		Grade Level Reading
		Hospitality Ministry	Elementary		
		Culinary Ministry	Nursery		
		Decoration Ministry			
		Transportation Ministry			
		Parking & Security Ministry			

2020 New St. Hurricane Leadership Teams ©2020

New St. Hurricane MBC - A biblical service model to highlight functions of ministry service that has been aligned to mission and purpose.

Designing the right organizational system for your church requires the coordination of ministry structures that pair functions with purpose. This is where church growth steadily moves as ministry needs are adapted to the messaging of God's Word as presented in the context of the culture and the times.

Utilizing vocabulary such as evangelism, worship, prayer, teaching the Bible, repentance, confession, community, serving, spiritual growth, giving, discipleship, fellowship, servant leadership, planning, evaluating, team building, and discipline support functions that are timeless and eternal to the message of scripture.

New St. Hurricane MBC Biblical Service Model

A Biblical Service Model to Highlight Functions of Ministry Service to Mission and Purpose. The Service Model has functioned at the church significantly well since near 2018. [97]

MARGARETTE W. WILLIAMS, ED.D., PH.D.

Ministry Accountability Flow Chart

New St. Hurricane Ministries
Monthly Accountability Chart

Who Does What & When?

Management operates best when all team members are aware of the accountability factors for WHO Does WHAT & WHEN. WHO answers to person or persons responsible for a specific task. WHAT asks of the nature of the responsibility. WHEN gives the time in terms of days or weeks to complete the task. Additionally, all persons know who is accountable for what.

Goals don't get accomplished on time when no one is driving them? There should be only *one* person assigned as the completer for all major project tasks. An organizational chart with roles and responsibilities clarified is called an **accountability chart**. All members of the team are aware of the order of responsibility.

Providing answers to the WHO Does WHAT & WHEN questions will eliminate frustration and promote timely quality outcomes.

Who decides what will be accomplished? Who takes ownership over individual parts? Who provides closure for finalizing the end results of the service project?

Steps for Completing NSH Monthly Accountability Chart:

MINISTRY: Write the name of the ministry on the form.
MONTH: Indicate what month the activity is taking place (Each form has 3 activity charts which represents one quarter of the year, ministries should have four reports by the end of year).
ACTIVITY: Write in the activity the ministry will be doing or participating in.
COMPLETED BY: Indicate the person or persons responsible for the project.
DATE: Indicate the date the activity will take place.
SERVICE RESULTS: Write in key components of the activity (how, what, where, and when).
Please turn in quarterly reports to Pastor Easter's Administrative Office

©Copyright 2018. Transformational Consultants Institute (TCI).
Margarette W. Williams, Ph.D., Ed.D.,Pine Bluff, AR 71601

Answers Who Does What & When (Williams)[98]

154

New St. Hurricane Ministries
Monthly Accountability Chart

Ministry_____

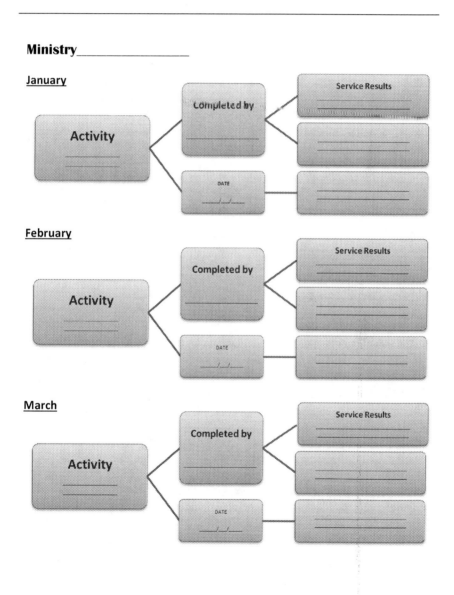

January

Activity

Completed by

DATE

Service Results

February

Activity

Completed by

DATE

Service Results

March

Activity

Completed by

DATE

Service Results

©Copyright, 2018, Transformational Consultants Institute (TCI), Margarette W. Williams, EdD, PhD.

New St. Hurricane Ministries
Monthly Accountability Chart

Ministry_____

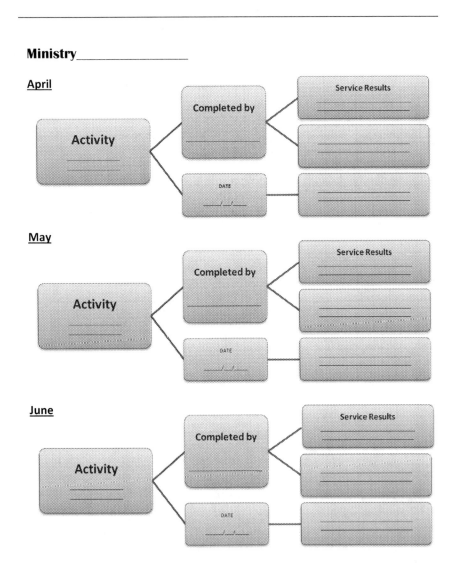

©Copyright, 2018, Transformational Consultants Institute (TCI), Margarette W. Williams, EdD, PhD.

New St. Hurricane Ministries
Monthly Accountability Chart

Ministry_____

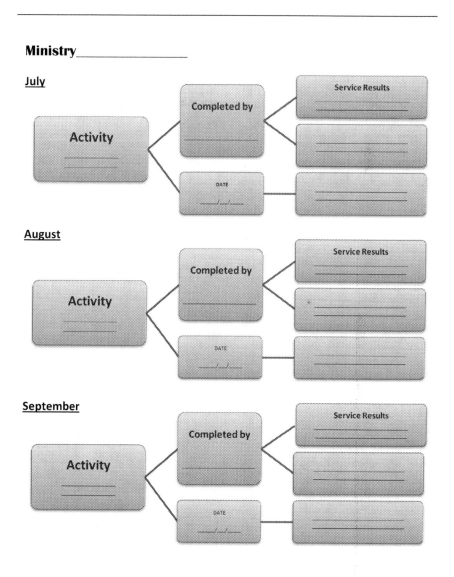

July

August

September

©Copyright, 2018, Transformational Consultants Institute (TCI), Margarette W. Williams, EdD, PhD.

New St. Hurricane Ministries
Monthly Accountability Chart

Ministry_____

October

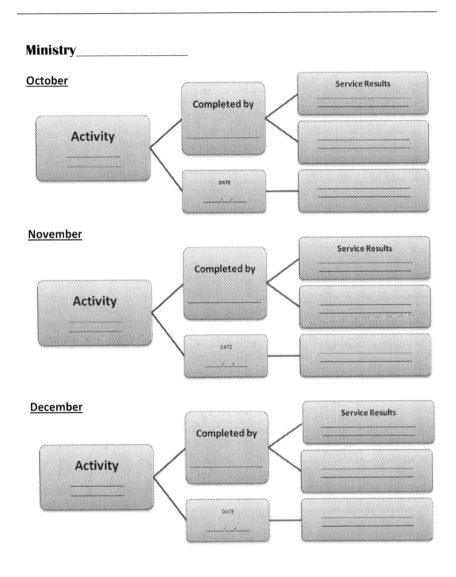

November

December

©Copyright, 2018, Transformational Consultants Institute (TCI), Margarette W. Williams, EdD, PhD.

❖

CHAPTER TWELVE

Managing Transformation:
A Call to Transition
New Technologies, Global Pandemics, Revival, and Renewed Hope

When God Signals Shifts to Transition

An appropriate conclusion to a discussion that the church must maintain a singular focus on the message of the cross as God's only mission is a final declaration that the church exists that people may *know Christ.* This mission is central to doctrine, all teachings, and each engagement in operations for ministry. In obedience to the Great Head of the church, I submit a summary position leveraging truths to express how the church will maintain its obligations to honor, obey, and love Christ. The important things to remember are that lasting transformation is experienced *only* when the church is guided by the leading of the Holy Spirit and the truth of His Word; *to the Honor and Glory of God.*

There has been throughout this volume, a continuous refocus on the message "Where in the operation of the church is Jesus the Christ, God's beloved Son in whom He is well pleased?" This is the message God desires for the people of God as they assume daily tasks in leadership, management and administration. The energy of the research has been to shed light on the hypothesis that there indeed exists a difference between the mission of God and the mission God left for His people.

Managing the traditional church during my youth and young adult upbringing was somewhat, simple. There was Sunday School, Baptist Training

Union (BTU), or other training programs as mandated by denominational boards. We had general mission, mission circles, young people's departments, choirs, Vacation Bible School, Bible study, ushers, laymen (not necessarily junior laymen; boys groups were included within the youth departments), and general eleven o'clock worship. For the most part, this was basically the structure of most church operations. Church was complete with Easter, Christmas, Mother's Day, Youth Sunday, the once a year Annual Choir Concert and Pastor's Anniversary. This was church as defined by most Baby Boomers living today, their parents and possibly even their parents' parents.

District associations, state young people's conventions, state congress sessions and national congress meetings were giants in the minds of major church leaders and most progressive minded pastors. But one day life in the church changed.

A new generation of cultural and societal shifts in business and technology ushered in major adjustments for how church members perceived church to have meaning for their lives. Church was not church as we knew it during earlier times.

Teaching and preaching were perceived to carry value and substance from new frames of knowledge with application equal to the learning church members felt accustomed to receiving in the educational, business, technological, political and global platforms of life. A more knowledgeable and educated laity required teaching from a scholarly and learned clergy. The opening worship arts experience has been transformed from the lead choir marching into the sanctuary to the melodious *"Holy, Holy, Holy, Lord God Almighty"*[99] hymn to today's live orchestra styled bands, accompanying praise teams singing new, traditional, and sometimes, near 'rock' contemporary worship praise.

World changes have now become operational alterations for the church. Denomination affiliation is no longer revered. Many churches have changed their names to remove the denomination tag in efforts to attract and recruit new members, person who may not desire to follow a set system of denominational rules or distinguishing characteristics. These thoughts are lead in to new discussions for how church members articulate truths relating to what they believe about their faith.

Actually, present-day methodologies are of little effect to what Christ says the church is from yesterday, to today, and on to eternity. The simple, yet consuming truth is how will church management lead congregations to a continuous love for the *"work of the church"* while a new focus today may be on *"work in the church."* The narrative for *churches participating in the Act of Christ* will always be the permanent mission that shall not be amended.

Pastors continue to follow the mandate to feed the sheep and to watch over them with love and care. Members are no less required to submit to those who have rule and authority over their lives and to live motivated to give of themselves unselfishly for others. Enthusiasm to continue serious reverence and appreciation for the role church plays in the lives of believers lies in how a church moves to align contemporary management and transformational leadership theories with God's grand biblical narratives found in His Holy Word. Ideas and new ways of learning will foster greater opportunity for the church to seek new ways to correlate today's contemporary perspectives with a continuous hope in scripture.

The Church Obeys the Call to Transition

Modern day changes in society bring about new prospective for the contemporary church. Modifications to former traditional approaches should be amended to incorporate transformational leadership ministry into newer models of church management. Time means change. This popular yet true statement is testament to why this volume in transformational messaging for the church is important. Chapter twelve presents transitional support to aid churches contemplating adjustments in advancing methods to sustain ongoing spiritual growth and vitality for current and future worship and ministry engagements.

There are numerous reasons why ministry strategies in church operations should be awakened to a need to transition. While there are indeed negative assumptions attached to causes churches desire to change, the devotion to galvanize attention to *mission* is always the principle value associated with all positive goals in modern innovations.

When the church gathers its leadership and members to pursue initiatives to improve performance, it is seizing opportunities to address key issues that often require change to processes, to job roles, organizational systems and oftentimes, to methodologies. An added value for the church is the inclusion of the use of technology and the multiple platforms technology brings to communicating the gospel message to the masses in today's culture.

Even without a pandemic, as we are living in during the writing of Chapter Twelve, technology was providing invaluable service to the day to day operations as well as serving as the media outreach for church administration and evangelism. A special section will be included at the close of this chapter to address discipleship and evangelism in the church in the era of a global pandemic and the call of the post pandemic church.

The Bible Teaches About New Innovations?

Although everything in existence experiences change, we are comforted in knowing that there are no variances in God and that his promises are certain throughout all dispensations.

Bible Verses to Study during Times of Innovation & Transition[100]

> Jeremiah 29:11- (NIV) For I know the plans I have for you," declares the Lord, "plans to prosper you and not to harm you, plans to give you hope and a future.

> Joshua 1:9 - (NIV) Have I not commanded you? Be strong and courageous. Do not be afraid; do not be discouraged, for the Lord your God will be with you wherever you go.

> Deuteronomy 31:8 - (NIV) The Lord himself goes before you and will be with you; He will never leave you nor forsake you. Do not be afraid; do not be discouraged.

> Proverbs 3: 5-6 – (NIV) Trust in the Lord with all your heart and lean not on your own understanding; in all your ways submit to Him, and He will make your paths straight.

> Psalm 32:8 - (NIV) I will instruct you and teach you in the way you should go; I will counsel you with my loving eye on you.

> Malachi 3:6 – (NIV) I the Lord do not change. So you, the descendants of Jacob, are not destroyed.

2 Peter 3:9 – (NIV) The Lord is not slow in keeping his promise, as some understand slowness. Instead He is patient with you, not wanting anyone to perish, but everyone to come to repentance.

Hebrews 13:8 – (NIV) Jesus Christ is the same yesterday and today and forever.

Isaiah 43:19 – (NIV) See, I am doing a new thing! Now it springs up; do you not perceive it? I am making a way in the wilderness and streams in the wasteland.

James 1:17 – (NIV) Every good and perfect gift is from above, coming down from the Father of the heavenly lights, who does not change like shifting shadows.

Psalm 18:2 – (NIV) The Lord is my rock, my fortress and my deliverer; my God is my rock, in whom I take refuge, my shield and the horn of my salvation, my stronghold.

Romans 12:1-2- (NIV) Therefore, I urge you, brothers and sisters, in view of God's mercy, to offer your bodies as a living sacrifice, holy and pleasing to God—this is your true and proper worship. Do not conform to the pattern of this world, but be transformed by the renewing of your mind. Then you will be able to test and approve what God's will is—His good, pleasing and perfect will.

Philippians 4:6-8 – (NIV) Do not be anxious about anything, but in every situation, by prayer and petition, with thanksgiving, present your requests to God. And the peace of God, which transcends all understanding, will guard your hearts and your minds in Christ Jesus. Finally, brothers and sisters, whatever is true, whatever is noble, whatever is right, whatever is pure, whatever is lovely, whatever is admirable— if anything is excellent or praiseworthy—think about such things.

Margarette W. Williams, Ed.D., Ph.D.

Managing Transition for Lasting Transformation

*Change management provides sequential order
within all systems of organizations.*

The above statement indicates that process preparation is required to bring needed transformation for businesses and in organizations, including the church. Change is about "effect on people." Change indicates how they respond to incoming differences. In the end, change is how congregations in general and individual members specifically respond to new ways of sorting through what occurs within the environment of the church. If members are unsuccessful in their personal transitions, if they do not learn and embrace fresh purpose in serving, they will not experience long term success to carry through on new initiatives. When a church adopts and embrace action plans required of a new spiritual design model, the congregation will develop and grow from multiple streams of activation.

Initiatives that further enhance believers in the kingdom begin with assumptions that the status may quo no longer serves the needs of the church and its ministries. A spirit of renewal, one delivered by the guidance of the Holy Spirit, will inevitably produce real and lasting achievements in ministry organizational outcomes.

The goal is to always promote biblical messaging essential to church mission. Church transitioning of this manner produces lasting achievements to reaching God's eternal purpose for the people served. God honors His divine plans; His will is to bring them to pass. Regardless of changes in society, in the culture and with masses of people from varying walks of life, the mission of the church should always propel members to evolve to a place where their actions are in alignment with God's intended will. Modifications that simply move people or events from point to point may produce short term shifting. However, these motions in movement seldom evolve to the stage of lasting transformation in reaching long term kingdom goals. It is not simply in transitional movement within the church that matters, but rather in intent to purpose for mission that Jesus is exalted and God is glorified.

The question becomes "how do churches spiritually discern the most appropriate purposes and methods to transition for change and better yet, how will they incorporate valuable tools in measurements of assessment when needed?" *The journey to achieve a positive design in messaging in church trends, church culture, and healthy church operations is important in times of transition.*

The greatest value from this present study is that it has constructed new dialogue inclusive of approaches for churches to utilize as they advance in transforming their environments for spiritual growth and edification.

HONOR to the Great Head of the Church presents a new *"positional statement"* for church transformation as it combined, throughout the chapters, scripture for each position presented for the thesis. The hypothesis declared that the authority of God is supreme for all matters in church worship and ministry obligations. The declaration to proclaim an insistence that the church stays on message with a continued devotion to Christ is the ultimate challenge in the book. Churches are called upon to combine the message of God's mission with practical application in organizational leadership, administration, and management.

Church consultants are change agents who offer systematic methods in approaches congregations use when discerning the *"why"* and the *"why not"* for adopting change to transform ministry in the church. Observing to know the right spaces to initiate discussion leads to a readiness for answering the "where are we with our obligations to meet the challenges of these times?" As agents of change, church consultants offer skills appropriate to a wide range of thought and solutions to major planning in recommendations and suggestions. Their solutions range from sharing how a church begins the decision making process to start a renewed focus for change, to incorporating transitional alterations within the congregation and the community. Operating from the heart of God is basic to establishing outcomes to achieve quality solutions for all renewed engagements.

Church Management in the Age of Technology

Four years ago, in 2017, as a writer for *The Mission*, a Quarterly Mission Lesson Guide of the National Baptist Woman's Auxiliary, National Baptist Convention, USA, Inc., I was given a four week assignment to research and write on the topic "Modern Technology in the Christian World." The focus was to discuss the church's relatedness to technology in ministry and in worship. The sub themes were *technology, teaching and training*. Each of the four week's writings consisted of subtopics for the weekly devotion and lesson study. The following pages are rewrites of the four weeks' devotions and lessons on technology and the Christian community in the management of church operations at the time of the writings.

The following Devotional Messages and Mission Lessons were written by this author, Dr. Margarette W. Williams. They were published in the Mission Quarterly by the Woman's Auxiliary of the National Baptist Convention, USA, INC, Fourth Quarter Edition, 2017. The lessons were written prior to the 2020 Novel Coronavirus COVID 19 global pandemic. The statements were written with no knowledge as to how dependent the world would soon become on technology platforms for basic communication as a result of a pandemic. The church body of believers social distanced for all of 2020 and now on into 2021. Technology platforms have become a necessity in the home, in business, industry, in health professions, the world of politics, for schools, and yes, the church.[101]

Mission Fourth Quarter Topic:
Modern Technology in the Christian World
Focus: Technology, Teaching and Training

Margarette W. Williams, Week One
Mission Devotional Message: Be Wise
Scripture: Ephesians 2:10(KJV)
Prayer:

It is fitting that a study in modern technology for the Christian world should be tempered with a discussion for believers to walk wisely in both personal usage and as church congregants. Without a doubt, delivery in the diversity of technologically enhanced church ministries offer greater rewards to accomplishing the singular mission of the church. Designing today's ministries while successfully incorporating Information Technology (IT) into operational plans of church administration provides church leaders with awesome advantages. From improved communication capability, to building a greater sense of community, to enabling formidable growth in discipleship; the benefits of technology in the church are amazing. Pastors and church leaders consistently seek networking and marketing opportunities to advance their ministry worthiness within the context of church membership and on into the larger community.

However, technology brings with it certain issues directly related to implementation and accountability. For all of its intended good, there is a degree of negativism associated with it. Ephesians 2:10 reminds us that as the workmanship of Christ Jesus, we have been created in Him to walk in good works. Christ gave Himself for us that Grace would produce in us a quality of good, continually. With keen discernment and sound judgment, balance is needed to maintain wise implementation with every new use of technology formatted within the church.

Mission Lesson Week One – Defining and Reshaping Christianity
Study Text: Ecclesiastes 1:9-10 (KJV)

The Lesson

Technology is transforming lives at a rapid speed. Actually, the average person has little awareness as to how much technology is influencing all of life's existence for this present generation. What is obvious is that technology has become a serious engine that drives daily operational movement in all of business and industry. It has changed how people communicate and live. The use of the Internet paired with social media platforms present serious divide between those with an understanding of how technology works and those who are clueless. I do not remember living in a decade or reading of a time in history where individuals of similar age, near equal educational status and knowledgeable capabilities can be so disconnected from their immediate peers in what they know about technology than in these present times. A close family member who chooses not to use a Smartphone or have access to continuous navigation with a Tablet is generally and seriously disconnected from others in the same family who are included in the information gathering group.

New advances in technology platforms ranging from sending and receiving simple text messages to obtaining documentation receipts in retail sales via their mobile, to evaluating teaching and instructors at a national congress in real time, are unprecedented occurrences happening every day. The expression "back in the day" can refer to technology enhancements from just two years ago or less when referring to knowledge of what is advancing each day in Information Technology (IT). The whole world seemingly is moving at the speed of technology.

A technologically dependent society did not begin with the advent of computers, the Internet, Smartphones or Tablets. Technology has influenced culture since the beginning of time, including prehistoric days. Primitive technology usage consisted of handheld tools (flints) to start fires, spears used to hunt, tools to dig and peel skins from animals. These are man's earliest methods with technology; practical instruments to obtain desired results. Earlier methods in farming, navigating cargo across deep waters and searching articles in the library are all methodologies used to gain access to connect to information beyond ourselves.

Today's media platforms have significantly changed the way people conduct life and communicate with one another. Likewise, technology enhances the work of the church to serve as resource for God's glory. The point to observe is in the term *resource*. The author of Ecclesiastes, King Solomon, wrote of this in his old age; during a time in his life when wisdom trumped ambition over earlier meaningless pursuits from personal desires. King Solomon reminds us in the ninth and tenth verses of this first chapter that regardless of the depth of transition in medium or format for all of life, there is nothing new here. He writes in the text that *"what has been is what will be, and what has been done is what will be done, and there is nothing new under the sun. Is there anything of which one can say, "Look! This is something new? It was here already, long ago; it was here before our time."*

The church has included new innovative enhancements believed to benefit members by connecting them to each other and to improved efforts of church operation. These resources must be viewed only in regard to how they support effective worship and missional outcomes. Streaming Live on Facebook, on-line giving, reading of God's word from Smartphones or Tablets are simply functions of resource. They reflect the times and the believed benefits in enhancements for today's church. They are not the intended end but rather they can be identified as means to obtain the True and Living end. Ecclesiastes teaches that our eyes are turned toward God for real newness of life. Christ defined the message of Christianity for all of mankind at Calvary. While methods may evolve, the message remains the same.

Regardless to the change in presentation or method of performance, believers should recognize if new additions emerge as an attraction to messaging. The capacity to impact lasting change in the souls of man runs deeper. The good work from our inner most being comes from the Spirit of Grace to summon God's divine glory on behalf of others. A reliance on technology to simply reach people or to add numbers as worshippers will be short lived if the unchangeable King of all things old and new is not the purposeful center of each engagement.

Margarette W. Williams, Week Two
Mission Devotional Message: Be Discerning

Scripture: Romans 12:2 (NIV)

"Do not be conformed to this world, but be transformed by the renewal of your mind, that by testing you may discern what is the will of God, what is good and acceptable and perfect."(NIV)

It is commonly accepted that modern day changes in technology in society as well as the church are here to stay. In fact, the average person has not seen nor possesses the capacity to envision what is to come, even in the next decade with regard to technology advancements. New innovations are designed to strengthen the worship experience, to aid and equip leaders and to empower memberships for greater support and participation. However, all effects on ministry may not be considered positive. Attention now shifts from the perceived immediate advantages that such powerful tools bring to a congregation. When implemented correctly, rewards outweigh shortcomings. The key is to recognize and separate the modality of presentation from the message of experience. Understanding the power and will of God is to continually follow after His just and transformative purpose. Following Him is to allow for the manifestation of His Grace to flow abundantly throughout the lives of the membership. Pastors and church leaders recognize that vision for church mission is fulfilled when success with technology is assimilated into the life of the church to basically achieve spiritual goals. They recognize and incorporate technology for its intended purpose. That purpose is to assist outcomes leading to righteous living.

Mission Lesson Week Two – Negativity Surrounding Technology
Study Text: Matthew 24:14 (KJV)

The Lesson

In efforts to reach people beyond the walls of the congregation with the gospel message, churches are seeking new possibilities to expand the Sunday worship experience and to allow members to communicate in ways vastly different than previously provided. Over the past several decades many changes in technology enhancements have become drivers in the way churches conduct business and minister to the masses. Streaming video, e-giving and other emerging technologies are reshaping churches as religious leaders seek to attract outreach via innovative ways of thinking, worshiping and communicating with the larger society.

The church body has witnessed numerous advancements to effective management in operations connecting technology with membership. Yet there remain certain constants in Christian worship to reflect the traditions of the church; those customs include preaching the Word and administering sacraments. In relation to how people live daily, technology is shaping the church in significant ways. It is becoming more and more of an empowerment tool for both pastors and congregants.

According to a Berna Group survey, ninety-seven percent of pastors now use the Internet to find information compared with seventy-eight percent in 2000. Thirty-nine percent of pastors said they had a spiritual or religious experience via the Internet while only fifteen percent said the same in 2000. The only surveyed function of technology that did not grow among pastors over the same period was using the Internet to play video games. [102]

It is fairly easy to recognize the many ways technology supports church growth. Certainly, it would be difficult to imagine worship in the assembly without microphones, amplification, electronic keyboards or mixers. Although the hymn book may be located at the back of many pews, the congregation usually follows along written words set to huge screens positioned strategically for viewing of music and the sermon throughout the sanctuary. In recent decades, electronic technology has probably shaped the worship hour more than any other single occurrence within the congregation.

Obviously, technology usage enriches relationships and keeps members connected. It reaches the online community and adds new members from nearby as well as faraway places. There is however a focus for possible negative effects and subtle dangers technology and all its structures may have. A quality question to ask of churches must include: will these enhancements bring glory to God?

There are issues readily identified with the implementation of technology in the church. These concerns may include inadequate budget, lack of volunteers required of a quality technology program and few individuals in the congregation with technological know-how.

Areas of concern about overuse and overdependence on technology usage are central to conversation the church can engage in when discussing pros and cons about technology. Mental health professionals, educators, counselors, and parents engage in interesting discussions about factors such as alienation, addiction, potential for sin, and wasting time as being among a plethora of negatives associated with unproductive use of technology, both individually and as a body of believers.

People feel excluded from social events when they do not have Internet capability. Persons without email, access to Facebook or text capability, must be included in a call log or the personal contact group, or they will be left out of the dialogue loop.

Compulsive and obsessive behaviors can be the results of an overdependence on Internet usage. The need to be plugged in continually or to respond to the latest tirades on Twitter or Facebook can lead to unhealthy engagements with people, ideas and situations.

It is becoming so fashionable to tweet or send a text that people are often aggravated with the ring tone of the phone. The presumed need to multitask without thinking about what is occurring, leads to unnecessary and overused obligations to texting as a sure way to obtain a response. Actually, the dependence on mobile phones, wrist gadgets and arm apps can become quite overbearing.

Substantive discussion is needed to address how Facebook can be used to bring out the worst in people: jealousy, envy, pride, lust, and gossip, are among negative character traits.

Finally, sometimes *valuable time can be wasted* surfing on multiple websites. There is so much on the Internet that could be counter to doctrinal teaching of scripture. All kinds of unhealthy knowledge can be found at the stroke of the fingertips.

Margarette W. Williams, Week Three
Mission Devotional Message: Be Cautious

Scripture: Romans 10:17-18 (NLT)
"So faith comes from hearing; that is, hearing the Good News about Christ. But I ask, have the people of Israel actually heard the message? Yes, they have: "The message has gone throughout the earth and the words to all the world." (NLT).

The mission of the church is to preach the gospel of Jesus Christ to all, that lost men will come to know Him. Hearing and receiving the grand message of salvation is the only mission; the only purpose for the church. Unbelievers will not experience the saving knowledge of Christ if the message of redemption is not heard. Before man can believe, there must be something to accept as truth. That something is the Word of God. Faith leads a follower to trust and obey. Regardless of the method of delivery, whether it is conveyed in person, over the Internet, heard through the airways of modern podcast, television or through the radio, the gospel is the message heard unto repentance and deliverance.

For many churches, technology enables the marketing and automation of the Biblical mandate to preach Good News worldwide. It moves the church's commandment to a place where it operates smoothly and with efficiency. The caution is to never forget the purpose for worship. Technology is not the substitute for mission, it is the medium. Christ is the end.

Mission Lesson Week Three – Advancing Human Sin
Study Text: Hebrews 13:21 (KJV).

"Equip you with everything good that you may do his will, working in us that which is pleasing in his sight, through Jesus Christ, to whom be glory forever and ever. Amen."

The Lesson

A possible new pedagogy for Christian educators is the topic for how technology and social media impact faith, teaching, and Christian practice. A number of studies relate how technology enhances the worship experience, serves to provide smooth operations in management, and supports many functions of communication. Writers of church growth have however, shaped dialogue referencing possible negative outcomes resulting from an imbalance in the implementation in the use of the Internet to teaching doctrine in the church. Today's lesson explores the need to focus on the impact of technology on human spiritual formation. The lesson considers specifically, curriculum design for teaching with technology in the congregation. When teaching youth and also adult learners, leaders can benefit from discussions that evaluate instruction found with some technology curriculum. Will an Internet lesson lead learners away from scripturally based doctrinal teaching? Do problems exist that lead to error for human confusion and sin? Establishing right judgment for what to teach, how to present it, and how effective is the evaluation process to discern its worthiness is always an appropriate course of action. What should be considered as doctrinal sound in classes and in the assembly is a powerful position a church must establish for teaching with technology in the congregation.

For many churches, technology is a phenomenal addition to worship and Christian service. It is valuable to support how churches operate their business, increase their revenue, and gain new and consistent relationships with members and the larger community. As a result of technology, churches run smooth and capable daily operations. But difficulties with technology can also be widespread. Problems can occur that affect individual decision making related to worship, Bible study, and small group exchanges.

Where does the church stand in reference to how teaching from the Internet influences or hinders spiritual formation in the life of the believer? How does the church keep watchful eye on the impact technology can have on the human soul? The questions here are not presented as new inquiry. Every generation has had similar difficulties with accepting innovative or contemporary creativity that utilizes new tools of activity to enhance the human experience. With this latest explosion in our culture of all things technology, systematic dialogue paired with persistent biblical study will provide content conducive to shaping doctrinal truths for using technology to promote faith, teaching, and practice.

Margarette W. Williams, Week Four
Mission Devotional Message: Be Strong
Scripture: 2 Timothy 3:16-17 (KJV)
Prayer

If you have ever felt you could not win life's battles on your own, you are correct. You were never meant to succeed in life alone.

Writing this Second Epistle to the youthful pastor at the Church at Ephesus, the Apostle Paul gave final counsel to his young protégée to continue in faithful living in the teaching of sound doctrine. Paul advised his *son in the ministry* to seek patience amidst trails and to earnestly bear the mantle of boldness in his call to follow Christ. Paul recognized that Timothy suffered with timidity and apprehension. Regardless of his personal difficulties, he was urged to continue living a life pleasing to God. The admonition given was a reminder to conduct his life from a place of truth needful of his present existence, but also unto life everlasting. His call to faithful pastoral care qualified him to fight the good fight (Timothy 1:18, NIV) for every good work.

The benefits of God's promises are profitable for teaching, for correction, judgment, and instruction in righteousness. Perfecting these qualities moves the believer to connect to the measure of the stature of Christ's fullness.

This is the assurance that *Christians stand complete in the will of God*. It is a position established to determine spiritual fitness for the discharge of duty to the kingdom in this life. The caution here is "to continue thou in the things which you have heard." This is indeed true for these times. Believers can be assured that like Timothy they will be strengthened to stand strong in faithful service to the glorious gospel of the blessed God (Timothy 1: 11, NIV).

Mission Lesson, Week Four – Destroying or Enhancing the Quality of Life
Study Text: 1 Corinthians 10:23-33 (KJV)

The Lesson

Life today means living during a time when for every question or need that comes to mind, the answer can be found by searching the Internet. An endless number of web sites to a singular inquiry can lead to hours in accumulating information, including information overload. A person can complete high school; obtain the Bachelors, Masters, PhD Degrees, and acquire multiple certifications without leaving the office recliner or keyboard. There is little need for interaction, discussion, or reflection from others in the pursuit to access vast amounts of knowledge by way of technology. Church operations require the availability of technology as a means to accomplishing daily functions to produce and complete managerial tasks.

Technology is a necessity. But what happens to the spiritual vitality of a church when there is too much dependency on technology or when technology becomes a substitute for face to face discussions and relationship building? There should consistently be opportunity to channel conversation and dialogue between pastors and members as they to seek to bring balance to questionable situations. What cautions are there for vulnerable young people as the church relates to them the many dangers from online predators targeting the youth? There are numerous questions to answer when considering the world's overuse in mobile technology from all ages of users.

Research highlights a short attention span epidemic for users resulting from numerous social media and online searches. The church has a responsibility to lead or at least guide curious Internet members engaged in various online Bible study groups. Adequate opportunities should be provided for teachers and students to develop feedback that ensures web classes contain chat rooms with the availability to critique the learning. When is there a right time to say *"enough?"* Consider what God's Word says about issues worthy of discussion relating technology to use in the church. Here is a list of topics church leaders can discuss about technology usage for curriculum, teaching, and worship.

1. Praise teams and praise dancers open worship with songs set to contemporary music.
2. On line Bible study groups, with or without feedback.
3. Consistent data status updates via Apps and Twitter during sermons and Bible teaching.
4. Constant in time placement of new status information on Facebook.
5. The shift in the traditional definition of "community in the church."
6. Opportunities for mission in both in reach and outreach ministry.
7. Substitution of physical worship with listening to sermons online or from a favorite TV preacher. Is there a new normal for the term traditional worship? What does that mean?

The Apostle Paul gave an insightful model for practicing tolerance and exploring the limits of *"believer's freedom"* when determining what is permissible and what is beneficial as it relates to other believers. 1 Corinthians 10:23-33 (KJV) instructs that sometimes it is difficult to know when to defer to weaker believers as he provided a simple rule of thumb for both churches and individual learners. He determined that when making decisions, it is best to decide what is sensitive, what is gracious, and what is expedient. He noted that some actions may not be wrong in and of themselves, but constructed thought for the believer to wisely consider when engaging in actions that may not be in the best interest of others. Paul reminded his readers that freedom in Christ should not exist at the risk of hurting others. When the question that follows is "Why should a person limit his actions by another person's conscience," the answer is to always determine if the actions bring glory and honor to God.

A Backward Look in Time

The church and the entire world have experienced serious and unspeakable challenges and changes since the onset of the global pandemic. From the early months of 2020 and on to the present, long held traditional values in technology usage in the church community, are now at least, questionable. It is obvious from the previous topics presented for the Mission lessons and the messaging from the writings herein that no thought was conceived of an occurrence of this magnitude to be thrust upon the earth. So much is different and quite adequately so has the church needed to depend on the use and support of all platforms in technology. The mandate to carry out the message of Matthew 28:18-20 is now conducted from within the wires of Wi-Fi and the multiple forms of Socia Media from all types of technological devices. Worship, teaching, preaching, Bible study, and for most congregations, all facets of church services have been conducted on-line for the past year. These platforms of forced-to-live-by resources have become the "new normal for teaching, preaching, and evangelism."

What a difference a day in time will make? Services for in reach, outreach community mandates to feed the poor, care for the sick and the forgotten, have all been mandated by church leaders via technology application. The world and surely the church are in awe of the majestic power of God's vastly deep and wide sovereignty to structure all of life as He wills and directs.

Church and Technology in the Age of Global Pandemics

It has been established that the use of new forms of technology in the church has positive outcomes for advancing God's Word beyond the centralized settings of the local worship church edifice. Because the mission of the church is to guide persons who do not know Christ, to seek Him; this singular purpose has become the driving force behind platforms designed for today's ministry. A central question to answer is *"how does the transforming church hold true to historic creeds and confessions, doctrine, repentance, and deliverance from sin while walking in tolerance to new and engaging advancements in technology?"*

Leaders of churches view this defining moment as opportunity to set strategies that continue to enable pastors to lead and disciple people to the love of God's Word and worship to Him during and after a global pandemic. The church is now tasked to seek maximum use of new ways of evangelizing to reach the lost, in teaching the will of God, and in sharing God's love within the community and around the world. God is still unfolding His grand design to eternal restoration for us every day. What is important is that the church continues to press toward a listening ear to hear what the Spirit is saying in this hour, at this moment, in this year of the Novel Coronavirus COVID 19 global pandemic and beyond.

We live separately in our homes, and rightfully so. Attempts to close down major sectors of the country have proven in the earlier months to be disturbing and lacking in decisive leadership from the government. Business owners ceased operations and many businesses that closed temporarily, may not open again. Basic management procedures came to a screeching halt during the early days of the pandemic here in the United States and across the globe. The economy was changed, in some cases changed forever. Jobs were lost. Families grieve the loss of loved ones. Health care disparities became major issues for poor and noninsured people. Restaurants all across the country suffered great loss in business and revenue. Schools closed and even as I write in this moment, federal oversight, administrators, teachers, and parents are struggling to establish solid ground rules to effectively manage schools for educating students during this school year in into the coming academic sessions. Everything has changed.

Numerous long held traditions of operations in church leadership, administration, and management were discontinued for a significant period of time. A common thought seemingly held by many great leaders, pastors, and theologians today is that some of these changes are permanent. Remarkable enough are facts that some of these familiar ways in tradition may be gone to be replaced by a new focus and new norms. Daily practices that established new ways of existing propelled insight for churches seeking to further their operations in worship, fellowship, and relationship building.

What has not changed is the mandate from our Lord Christ to the church to "go and make disciples of all nations (Matthew 28:1, NIV)." Disciple making is essential to the continued edification of church growth, restoration, evangelism, and many relational emphases connected to upcoming values for the future. When many culturally present ways of conducting church business have long been exchanged for newer ways of worship and serving; giving way to new styles in methodologies and the many platforms of technologies available, some things will remain throughout the ages. Thank God for a call to renewed emphasis on revival, evangelism for the lost, and a refocus to disciple God's people who have been redeemed from the world to a calling to honor the great Head of the Church, our Lord, Jesus, the Christ.

As a final statement, I close with a November 2020 Mission Lesson written and published in the Mission Study Guide months after the start of the pandemic. This final lesson summarizes concluding expectations for the church as relating to the promises of continued hope in revival from our Lord,

Christ. With this ending thought, the message remains that Christ, the Great Head of the Church, is due all Honor unto Him.

November 2020
Lesson Four
What God Wants

Study Text: Deuteronomy 10:12-14, (KJV)
Objective: *To know and do the will of God…regardless of the circumstances or the situation.*

THE LESSON

For such a time as this! "He, who has an ear, let him hear what the Spirit is saying to the church, (Revelation 3:22, KJV)." Deuteronomy, the fifth book of the Pentateuch, written by Moses, the Hebrew prophet, teacher, and leader of God's people, has been described as a book of *transition*. Listed here are several definitions for the word transition: *change, evolution, switch, alteration or shift.* Basic to most conversations on spiritual matters, it is generally assumed that God is *shifting things in this present atmosphere.* In this pandemic season of the Novel Coronavirus God is moving with intentionality within the universe. I believe I am safe to say that never before in the lifetime of most persons living today has an experience of this magnitude been evident to reveal God manifesting Himself in the manner He has done so during the 2020 COVID-19 year.

Revolutionary occurrences of unprecedented proportions are upon mankind, from government to the financial infrastructures of the world, from the full scope of academia to the towers of huge economical world market enterprises. Life prior to the onset of this disastrous pandemic appeared to be far from the realities the world seems to face today. From the edifices for church worship centers, both grand and small, to the humble styles in worship and teaching of God via technology platforms, as a result of the need for social distancing; life has changed.

A phrase to explain the times for the day could be *"BC and AC, Before COVID 19 and After COVID 19."* So much has changed. Here again, I believe that a lot of what has been lost will not return. You hear words like "this is the new normal" to which, society will in many instances, be measured by life before the pandemic and life after the pandemic. Questions church leaders are asking and seeking answers to center around the knowledge that God is moving the church to a new level of worship, fellowship, and service to Him in the kingdom. Primarily, pastors and denominational leaders are struggling to put into focus quality solutions and answers to "what the church will look like post COVID-19."

Yet, there is one central theme that seems to permeate through all conversations and discussions thus far. That is, the church body of believers is now without a doubt aware, if there was not a clear focus before, of who makes up the church. The church edifice, the brick and mortar sanctuary, the little church house building or even the great grand cathedral; none of these structures *are the church*. They are God's places of worship where He seeks to meet His church in one accord to worship and hear from Him. The people of God are His church. Pastors continue to lead, feed and shepherd the church. As I write today, many pastors continue to carry out their commissions from their homes to the homes of their congregations, *the people of God*.

At the time of the writing in Deuteronomy Chapter Ten, Israel was also experiencing a shifting into a new life changing experience; a new culture. Israel was preparing to enter the Promised Land, overtake the inhabitants there, and establish a new way of life, one far from the bondage of Egypt and most definitely, far from the forty years of wandering in the wilderness. God's plan for His beloved Israel was for a new focus centered on worship and service to the one true living God. He commanded that their living would be reflective of His nature and His character.

The Israelites had been set apart for God's holy purposes. Above all the nations on earth, they were chosen to be a peculiar people set apart and dedicated to the worship and service of God. The church today is likewise, set apart as God's holy people, [set apart] unto the Lord, as His light shining in a dark world. Just as God commanded the Israelites to love and worship Him alone, so is it today, that the twenty-first century church is also dedicated to worship, serve, and most importantly, to give all honor and glory to our Lord, the Great Head of the Church.

ENDNOTES

Chapter One

1 Christopher J. H. Wright, *The Mission of God,* (Downers Grove: IVP Academic, 2006).

2 Christopher J. H. Wright, *The Mission of God, 31.*

3 J. Sidlow Baxtor, *Explore the Book In One Volume* (Grand Rapids: Zondervan Publishing House, 1971).

4 Ibid.

5 John R. Piper, *Desiring God: Meditations of a Christian Hedonist,* (Colorado Springs: Multnamah Publishers, 2011).

6 Westminister Assembly, *Westminister Confession of Faith,* A Reformed Confession of Faith. Church of England, Westminister Standard. www.*wikipediA.org, 1646.*

7 Matthew George Easton, *Easton's Bible Dictionary,* (Oxford: CreateSpace Independent Publishing Platform, 2017).

8 Orville J. Nave, *Nave's Topical Bible,* (Peabody: Hendrickson Publishers, 2002).

9 National Baptist Statement of Faith, http://www.nationalbaptist.com/about-us/what-we-believe.html, accessed February 16, 2021.

10 Bethlehem Baptist Church Statement of Faith, Bethlehem Baptist Church, Minneapolis, MN.

Chapter Two

11 Dr. William J. Shaw, *"The Heavenly Vision, the Mission of the Church,"* Congress Study Guide, National Baptist Congress of Christian Education, Nashville: Sunday School Publishing Board, 2010.

12 Dr. Forrest Harris, *"Theological Claims for Christian Mission and Practices.* Congress *Study Guide,* National Baptist Congress of Christian Education, Nashville: Sunday School Publishing Board, 2010.

13 Dr. Elliott Cuff, *"Converting Mission Minded-less Churches to the Mission of Jesus Christ,"* Congress Study Guide. National Baptist Congress of Christian Education, Nashville: Sunday School Publishing Board, 2010.

Chapter Three

14 *Sola Scriptura*, The meaning of "By scripture alone," http://www.en.m.wikipedia.org.

15 Don Stewart, "In What Sense is the Bible the Inspired Word of God.cgm?" www.blueletterbible.org/Comm/steward_don/faq/bible-authoriative-word/wuestion2-is-the-bible, 2021.

16 John Macarthur, "The Sufficiency of Scripture," *Our Sufficiency in Christ*, (Dallas: Word, 1991), 75-90.

17 Herbert L. Samworth, "Tyndale's Plougboy," www.tyndalesploughboy.org, 2019.

18 Sarah Bryson, "William Tyndale," http://www.tudorsociety.com, 2015.

19 John M. Brentnall, "Henry Bullinger and the Exposition of Scripture," www.bibleleaguetrust.org, 2021.

20 Rainer, Thom S. & Geiger, Eric, *Simple Church,* (Nashville: B&H Publishers, 2006).

21 Ibid

22 Anthony, Michael J. & James Estep, Jr., *Management Essentials for Christian Ministries,* (Nashville: B&H Publishers, 2005).

Chapter Four

23 Scripture references, "Who Jesus is as it relates to the Church," *http://bibleknowing-jesus.com.*

24 Scripture references, "Know Christ as Head of the Church," *http://bibleknowing-jesus.com*

25 Eliff, Bill, "Who is the Head of the Church?" Church Leadership, www, http://lifeaction.org, 2018.

26 Ibid.

27 Maxwell, John, *Developing the Leader Within You 2.0,* (Nashville: Thomas Nelson Publishers, 1993).

28 Kevin, Kruse, "What is Leadership?" http://www.forbes.com. 2013

29 Cohen, William, A., "Drucker on Leadership," First edition, (Hoboken, Jessey-Bass, 2009).

30 Warren, G. Bennis, "Leadership Experience to Develop Leaders," http://www.schholar.google.com, 1971-77.

31 Michael Schwantes, "Bill Gates Explains What Separates Successful Leaders from Everyone Else in Two Words." Icons & Innovators, http://www.inc.com, 2020.

32 John Maxwell. *Developing the Leader Within You 2.0.* (Nashville: Thomas Nelson Publishers, 1993

33 Bill Lawrence, "Foundational Principles of Leadership," http://www.Bible.org. Senior Professor Emeritus of Pastoral Ministries and Adjunct Professor of DMin Studies, Dallas Theological Seminary, 2007.

34 Brooks Faulkner, "Seven Biblical Models of Leadership," https://www.lifeway.com/en/articles/church leadership-seven-biblical-models, 2014.

Chapter Five

35 Geoffrey V. Guns, *Understanding Spiritual Leadership Authority: A Practical and Biblical Model for Today's Church* Leaders, (Virginia Beach: Geoffrey V. Guns Publishing, 2002).

36 Alexander Strauch, *Biblical Eldership,* (Colorado Springs: Lewis & Roth Publishers, 2003).

37 Scripture passages, "Pastoral Leadership for the church," *https://bible.org/seriespage/lesson-53-job- description-church-leaders-acts-2028*

38 Margarette A. Williams, "Informed Consent Letter to Pastors."

39 Margarette A. Williams, "Eight Question Survey for Pastors."

40 Geoffrey V. Guns, *Understanding Spiritual Leadership Authority: A Practical and Biblical Model for Today's Church Leaders,* (Virginia Beach: Geoffrey V. Guns Publishing, 2002).

41 Ibid.

Chapter Six

42 Oswald Sanders, *Spiritual Leadership*, (Chicago: Moody Press, 2007).

43 Mile Ayers, *Power to Lead: Five Essentials for the Practice of Biblical Leadership,* First Edition, (Columbia Station: RBK Publishing Group, 2015).

44 Scripture references, "Equip and Train Leaders for Service," http://www.bible.knowing- jesus,com/topics/Equipping,-Spiritual

45 Williams, Scott, "Outreach and Missions Blog, Church leaders.com," http://www.churchleaders.com

46 Church leaders.com, "Being an example for others by following the example of Christ," https://trainchurchleaders.com/example.htm

47 John Maxwell. *Developing the Leader within You 2.0,* (Nashville: Thomas Nelson Publishers, 1993).

48 BrainyQuote.com, http://www.BrainyQuote.com Greek Philosopher Heraclitus. Born (544BC – 483 BC), in Ephesus, Anatolia, now Seljuk, Turkey.

49 Kenneth L. Swetland, *Facing Messy Stuff in the Church,* (Grand Rapids: Kregel Academic & Professional, 2005).

50 Edmonson, Ron, "Three Simple Steps to Reproduce Church Leadership," http://www.ronedmondson.com,2014.

51 Edmonson, Ron, "Ten Ways to Develop a Culture of Recruitment," http://www. ronedmonson.com, 2018.

Chapter Seven

52 Adkins, Todd, "Is Your Church Plugging Holes or Reproducing Leaders," http:// www.CHURCHLEADERS.com, 2017.
53 Ibid.
54 Rainer, Thom S. & Stetzer, Ed, *Transformational Church: Creating a New Scorecard for Congregations,* (Nashville: B&H Publishers, 2010).
55 Scripture references, "Servant Leadership Empowerment for the Church," https://www.biblestudytools.com/topical-verses/bible-verses-about-servant-leadership/, 2020.
56 Greenleaf, Robert K, "The Servant as Leader," https://www.greenleaf.org/ what-is-servant-leadership/,1970.
57 Robert E. Greenleaf Center for Servant Leadership, https://www.greenleaf.org/ blog/ 2020.
58 Proofhub blog, "7 Leadership Styles: Which Type of a Leader are You?" https:// blog.proofhub. 2018.
59 Scripture references, "Transforming Life through the Word," https://www. biblestudytools.com/topical-verses/bible-verses-about-transformation/, 2020.

Chapter Eight

60 Scripture references, "Teamwork in the Bible," https://www.biblestudytools. com/topical-verses/bible-verses-about-teamwork/, 2020.
61 Philip Nation, "Essentials for Creating a Disciples Making Culture in Your Church," Facts and Trends Magazine https://lifewayresearch.com/2013/04/02/ essentials-for-creating-a-disciple-making-culture-in-your-church, 2013.
62 Geiger, Eric, Kelley, Michael, & Nation, Philip. *Transformational Discipleship: How People Really Grow.* (Nashville: B&H Publishers, 2012).
63 Ibid.
64 Steve Murrell, "Essentials for Creating a Disciples Making Culture in Your Church." Facts and Trends Magazine, https://lifewayresearch.com/2013/04/02/ essentials-for-creating-a-disciple-making-culture-in-your-church/, 2013.
65 Ferguson, Jon, "Essentials for Creating a Disciples Making Culture in Your Church," Facts and Trends Magazine, https://lifewayresearch.com/2013/04/02/ essentials-for-creating-a-disciple-making-culture-in-your-church/, 2013.
66 Godwin Sathianatha, "Grow a Disciple-Making Culture in Your Church." https:// www.thegospelcoalition.org/article/how-to-grow-a-disciple-making-culture-in-your-church/,2013.

Chapter Nine

67 Ventura, Steve & Templin, Michelle Correia, *"Five Star Teamwork. How to Achieve Success..TOGETHER*, 1st Edition. Bedford: Walk the Talk Publisher, 2005.

68 Beich, Elaine, *The Pfeiffer Book of Successful Team-Building Tools: Best of the Annuals 1ˢᵗ Edition*. (Hokoken:Pfeiffer, 2007).

69 Key Elements of an Effective Church Administration, An Essay, (Bartleby Research, 2016). http://www.bartleby.com

70 Ibid.

71 Free Church Forms, https://www.freechurchforms.com/pastor job description. html

72 Margarette W. Williams, "New St. Hurricane Missionary Baptist Church Pastoral Job Description," New St. Hurricane MBC, 3319 South Ohio Street, Pine Bluff, AR 71601, 2012.

Chapter Ten

73 Stetzer, Ed. & Rainer, *Transformational Church: Creating a New Scorecard for Congregations*, (Nashville:B&H, 2010).

74 Ed Stetzer, "Three Signs of a Transformation Church," Daily Digest, Stetzer, https://outreachmagazine.com/features/4688-3-signs-of-a-transformational-church.html, 2015.

75 Jennie B. Wilson, *"Lyrics to Hold to God's Unchanging Hand,"* https://hymnary.org/text/timeisfilledwithswifttransition, 1906, public domain.

76 Scripture references, "God's Word and Church Growth,"https://www.biblestudytools.com/topical-verses/bible- verses-about-growth/, 2020.

77 Margarette A. Williams, *"Organizational Change, Strategic Leadership and Decision Making at the National Baptist Congress of Christian Education,"* (PhD Diss, Trinity Theological Seminary, 2013.)

78 Margarette A.Williams, "Vision and the Management of Change," *A Position Paper,* (PhD Program, Trinity Theological Seminary, 2010.)

79 Sullivan, Gordan & Harper, Michael V, *Hope is Not a Method: What Business Leaders Can Learn from America's Army,* (New York: Currency/Regency Random House, 1997).

80 Margaerette A. Williams, "Vision and the Management of Change," *A Final Research Paper, (*PhD Program, Trinity Theological Seminary, 2012.)

81 Anthony, Michael J. & Estep, James Jr, *In Management Essentials for Church Ministries,* (Nashville: B&H Publishers, 2005).

82 Scripture references, "What the Bible Says about Vision for the church." https://www.biblestudytools.com/topical-verses/bible-verses-about-vision/, 2020.

83 Aubrey Mulphur, "Developing a Vision: What Kind of Church Would We Like to Be?" *Advanced Strategic Planning*, (Nashville: B& H Publishers, 2013).

84 Piatt, Jason, Developing a Vision for Your Operations: 7 Steps to See Where You are Headed, https://www.industryweek.com/operations/article/22008164/developing-a-vision-for-your-operations-7-steps- to-see-where-you-are-headed, Assessed, 2020.

Chapter Eleven

85 Tiffany C. Wright, "Principles of Organizational Theory," https://smallbusiness.chron.com/principles-organizational-theory, 2015.

86 Emerald Works, "Fiedler's Contingency Model: Matching Leadership Style to a Situation," Mind Tools Content Team, Essential Skills for an Excellent Career, https://www.mindtools.com/pages/article/fiedler.htm, 2020.

87 Bernard, Pierre & Deschamps, Marc, "The Birth of Modern System Theory," https://www.researchgate.net/publication/329362976/Kalman1960Thebirth ofmodernsystemtheory,1960

88 Scripture references, "God's Word and Organizational Theory," https://bible.knowing-jesus.com/topics/Organization, 2020.

89 Margarette W. Williams, "Applied Theories in Human and Organizational Development." A Position Paper, (PhD Program, Trinity Theological Seminary, 2011.)

90 Ibid.

91 Papalia, Diane E. Olds, Sally Wendkos, Feldman, Ruth Duskin, *Human Development,* (New York: McGraw Hill Publishers, 2005).

92 Grangel, Kenneth O. & Wilhoit, James C, *The Christian Educators' Handbook on Spiritual Formation,* (Wheaton: Victor Books-A Division of Scripture Press Publications, Inc, 1994).

93 Ibid.

94 Rothwell, William J., Sullivan, Roland L., & McLean, Gary N, *Practicing Organizational Development: A Guide for Consultants, 1ˢᵗ Edition,* (Hoboken: Pfeiffer Publishing, 1995).

95 Margarette W. Williams, *"New St. Hurricane MBC Organizational Flow Chart,"* Transformational Consultants Institute (TCI), Church Consulting Service, 2017.

96 Margarette W. Williams, *"2017 New St. Hurricane MBC Leadership Teams Organizational Structure,"* Transformational Consultants Institute (TCI), Church Consulting Service, 2017.

97 Margarette W. Williams, *"2018 New St. Hurricane MBC Leadership Teams Organizational Structure."* Transformational Consultants Institute (TCI), Church Consulting Service, 2018.

98 Margarette W. Williams, *"New St. Hurricane MBC Monthly Accountability Chart,"* Transformational Consultants Institute (TCI), Church Consulting Service. 2020.

Chapter Twelve

99 Reginald Heber, "Holy, Holy, Holy, Lord God Almighty," Lyrics, Public Domain, https://hymnary.org 1826,

100 Scripture references, " Bible verses for times of transition and change," https://www.openbible.info/topics/transition_and_change, 2020.

101 Williams, Margarette W, "Mission Study Guide: Fourth Quarter," *Devotional Messages and Mission Study, Woman's Auxiliary to the National Baptist Convention, USA, Inc,* Nashville: Sunday School Publishing Board, 2017.

102 Jonathan Merritt, "Why Technology Didn't and Won't Destroy the Church," Berna Survey, https://religionnews.com/2015/02/27/technology-hasnt-wont-destroy-church/, 2015.

WORKS CITED

The list of references is included for further study into a deeper understanding on the topics of this present publication. As noted in the opening section of the book, a reference was given to indicate that resources from religious and secular publications ranging in contributions from academia to industry, to politics, and the social sciences would be included as valuable to exploring a fuller scope in knowledge on the four sections of the book. Each reader should explore the relatedness of their worth for personal usage in an individual study.

Section 1:
Transforming God's Church for His Mission

Baxter, J. Sidlow. Explore the Book. In One Volume. 10th Printing. Grand Rapids: Zondervan. 1971.

Blackaby, Henry T. & King, Claude V. Experiencing God. How to Live the Full Adventure of Knowing and Doing the Will of God. Nashville: B&H Publishing Group. 1994.

Conyers, A. J. A Basic Christian Theology. Nashville: B&H Publishing Group. 1995.

Evans, Tony. God's Glorious Church. The Mystery and Mission of the Body of Christ. Chicago: Moody Press. 2003.

Guthrie, Shirley C. *Christian Doctrine.* Louisville, KY: Westminster John Knox Press, 2018.

MacArthur, John. A Simple Christianity. Rediscover the Foundational Principles of Our Faith. 1995.

Migliore, Daniel L. *Faith Seeking Understanding.* Grand Rapids, MI, MI: William B. Eerdmans, 1991.

Wright, Christopher J. H. The Mission of God: Unlocking the Bible's Grand Narrative. Downers Grove: IVP Academic. 2006.

Wright, Christopher J. H. The Mission of God's people: A Biblical Theology of the Church's Mission. Grand Rapids: Zondervan. 2010.

Section 2:
A Transformational Model for Leadership

Bambrick-Santoyo, Paul. Leverage Leadership. A Practical Guide to Building Exceptional Schools. San Francisco: Jossey-Bass. 2012.

Berkley, James D. Leadership Handbook of Outreach and Care. Practical Insight from a Cross Section of Ministry Leaders. Grands Rapids: Baker Books. 1994.

Blackaby, Henry & Richard. Spiritual Leadership. Moving People on to God's Agenda. Nashville: B&H Publishing Group. 2011.

Blanchard, Ken. The Heart of a Leader. Insights on the Art of Influence. Colorado Springs: David C. Cook. 2007.

Blanchard, Ken & Hodges, Phil. The Servant Leader. Transforming Your Heart, Head, Hands, & Habits. Nashville: Thomas Nelson. 2003.

Geiger, Eric & Peck, Kevin. Designed to Lead. The Church and Leadership Development. Nashville: B&H Publishing Group. 2016.

Guns, Geoffrey V. Setting the House in Order. A Guide for Leading Change in the Local Church. Virginia Beach: Bright Hope Publishing Company. 2004.

Guns, Geoffrey V. Understanding Spiritual Leadership Authority. Practical and Biblical Model for Today's Church Leaders. Virginia Beach: Geoffeey V. Guns. 2002.

Halcomb, James, Hamilton, David, Malmstadt, Howard. Courageous Leaders. Transforming Their World. Seattle: YWAM Publishing. 2000.

Hull, Bill. *The Disciple-Making Pastor: Leading Others on the Journey of Faith*. Grand Rapids, MI, MI: Baker Books, 2007.

Lawrenz, Mel. *The Dynamics of Spiritual Formation*. Grand Rapids, MI, MI: Baker Books, 2000.

Marion, Russ. Leadership in Education. Orzanizational Theory for the Practitioner. Upper Saddle River: Merrill Prentice Hall. 2002.

Maxwell, John C. Developing the Leader within You. Nashville: Thomas Nelson. 1993.

Maxwell, John C. Developing the Leader within You. The Workbook. Nashville:Thomas Nelson.2001.

Milco, Michael R. Ethical Dilemmas in Church Leadership. Case Studies in Biblical Decision Making. Grands Rapids: Kregel. 1997.

Kouzes, James M. & Posner, Barry Z. The Leadership Challenge. How to Keep Getting Extdrordinary Things Done in Organizations. San Francisco: Jossey- Bass Publishers.1995.

Kouzes, James M. & Posner, Barry Z. The Leadership Challenge. The Workbook. San Francisco: Jossey-Bass Publishers. 2003.

Rainer, Thom S. & Geiger, Eric. Simple Church. Nashville: B&H Publishing Group. 2006.

Richards, Larry, and Clyde Hoeldtke. Church Leadership: Following the Example of Jesus Christ. Grand Rapids, MI, MI: Zondervan, 1988.

Sanders, J. Oswald. Spiritual Maturity: Principles of Spiritual Growth for Every Believer. ChIcago, IL: Moody Publishers, 2007.

Sanders, Oswald J. Spiritual Leadership. Principles of Excellence for Every Believer. Chicago: Moody. 2007.

Spence, Gerry. How to Argue and Win Every Time. New York: St. Martin's Press. 1995.

Section 3:
A Transformational Model for Administration

Deskins, Janet L. Effective Church Administration. The Church Administrator's Guidebook. 2nd Edition. Rev. Dr. J. L. Deskins. 2018.

LaMothe-Lassey, Sapphira. The Unstoppable Church. An Effective Guide to Church Administration. HFW Publishing. 2018.

MacArthur, John. *The Master's Plan for the Church.* Chicago, IL: Moody Publishers, 2008.

Odom, Jeremy W. A Pastor's Introduction to Church Administration. Administering the 21st Century Church Effectively. Natchitoches: Big O Publishing. 2016.

Powers, Bruce. Church Administration Handbook. Nashville: B&H Publishing Group. 2008.

Rothwell, William L., Sullivan, Ronald, McLean, Gary N. Practicing Organization Development. A Guide for Consultants. San Francisco: Jossey-Bass Pheiffer.1995.

Tidwell, Charles A. Church Administration Effective Leadership for Ministry. Nashville: Broadman Press. 1985.

Williams, Margarette W. Organizational Change, Strategic Leadership, & Decision Making at the National Baptist Congress of Christian Education. Ph.D. Dissertation in Ministry Leadership. Newburg: Trinity Theological Seminary. 2013.

Section 4:
A Transformational Model for Management

Anderson, Leith. A Church for the 21st Century. Bringing Change to your Church to Meet the Challenges of a Changing Society. Minneapolis: Bethany House Publishers. 1992.

Anthony, Michael J. & Estep, James Jr. Management Essentials for Christian Ministries. Nashville: B&H Publishers. 2005.

Beich, Elaine. The Pfeiffer Book of Successful Team-Building Tools. San Francisco: Jossey-Bass/Pfeiffer. 2001.

Dever, Mark, and Paul Alexander. *The Deliberate Church: Building Your Ministry on the Gospel.* Wheaton,, IL: Crossway Books, 2005.

Frost, Michael & Hirsch, Alan. The Shaping of Things to Come. Innovation and Mission for the 21st-Century Church. Grand Rapids: Baker Books. 2013.

Geiger, Eric, Kelley, Michael, & Nation, Philip. Transformational Discipleship. How People Really Grow. Nashville: B&H Publishing Group. 2012.

George, Carl F. & Logan, Robert E. Leading and Managing Your Church. Grand Rapids: Fleming H. Revell, a Division of Baker Book House Publishers. 1998.

Harris, Jim Ph.D. & Brannick, Joan Ph.D. Finding & Keeping Great Employees. New York: AMACOM. 1999.

Hendricks, Howard & William. As Iron Sharpens Iron. Building Character in a Mentoring Relationship. Chicago: Moody Press. 1995.

Kaye, Beverly & Jordan-Evans, Sharon. Love'em or Lose'em. Getting Good People to Stay. San Francisco: Berrett-Koehler Publishers, Inc. 1999.

Malphurs, Aubrey. Advanced Strategic Planning. A 21st Century Model for Church and Ministry Leaders. Grand Rapids: Baker Books. 2013.

Manchini, Will. Innovating Discipleship. Four Paths to Real Discipleship Results. Church Unique Intentional Leader Series. 2013.

Martin, Glen & McIntosh, Gary. The Issachar Factor. Understanding Trends that Confront Your Church and Designing a Strategy for Success. Nashville: B&H Publishers. 1993.

McNeal, Reggie. The Present Future. Six Tough Questions for the Church. San Francisco: Jossey-Bass. 2003.

Milano,Michael & Ullius, Diane. Designing Powerful Training. The Sequential- Interative Model. San Francisco: Jossey-Bass Pfeiffer. 1998.

Newstrom, John & Scannell, Edward. The Big Book of Team Building Games. New York: McGraw-Hill. 1998.

Phillips, Jack J. Accountability in Human Resource Management. Techniques for Evaluting the Human Resource Function and Measuring the Bottom-Line Contribution. Houston: Gulf Publishing Company.1996.

Robbins, Stephen P. & Decenzop, David A. Fundamentals of Management. Essential Concepts and Applications.Upper Saddle River: Pearson Prentice Hall. 2003.

Sterzer, Ed. & Rainer, Thom S. Transformational Church. Creating a New Scorecard for Congregations. Nashville: B&H Publishing Group. 2010.

Stetzer, Ed. & Geiger, Eric. Transformational Groups. Creating a New Scorecard for Groups. Nashville: B&H Publishing Group. 2014.

Swetland, Kenneth L. Facing Messy Stuff in the Church. Case Studies for Pastors and Congregations. Grand Rapids: Kregel Publications. 2005.

Ulrich, Dave. Human Resource Champions. The Next Agenda for Adding Value and Delivering Results. 12 Vision Templates for Finding and Focusing Your Church's Future. Boston: Harvard Business School Press. 2016.

Wagner, C. Peter. Changing Church. How God is Leading His Church into the Future. Ventura: Regal. 2004.

Printed in the United States
by Baker & Taylor Publisher Services